I0840882

Elements:

Elemental, Elementary

by
The Lonesome Hillbilly

Books by the same author

The Book on Motorcycle Camping
How to Live on the Road Full Time

Places: I'm Going to Go Back There, Some Day

Roads: All Roads Lead to Roam

Friends: Two-Legs, Four-Legs, Six-Legs, Wings and Roots

Visions: Things and Ideas Found in the Wild

Elements: Elemental, Elementary

Things in Heaven and Earth
Essays from Places, Roads, Friends, Visions and Elements
with full-color illustrations

Dedicated to
Whoever created all of this
I very much appreciate it.
Thank you.

Contents

The Glories
by Rudyard Kipling
1925

In faiths and Food and Books and Friends
  Give every soul her choice.
For such as follow divers ends
  In divers lights rejoice.

There is a glory of the Sun
  ('Pity it passeth soon!)
But those whose work is nearer done
  Look, rather, towards the Moon.

There is a glory of the Moon
  When the hot hours have run;
But such as have not touched their noon
  Give worship to the Sun.

There is a glory of the Stars,
  Perfect on stilly ways;
But such as follow present wars
  Pursue the Comet's blaze.

There is a glory in all things;
  But each must find his own,
Sufficient for his reckonings,
  Which is to him alone.

Introduction: The Elements

The Ancients recognized four Elements: Earth, Air, Fire and Water. But they were speaking of the physical world, for there is also Spirit. It is different from, and senior to, the elements.

Look at the Earth, at the rocks and the soil. They rise from the depths as massive mountains, and crumble to boulders, rocks, gravel, sand, and end as silt in the sea. They compress and harden and reunite, then rise again, and again, and again. They bear neither the shapes nor the forms that they bore before, but we can still see them when we look with more than our eyes. Mountains, faces, rivers, fields, all come to light when we look and we dream. We see in Earth what we have put there to be seen, anything, everything, unlimited, infinite.

Gaze into the Air, and what do you see? Cerulean blue, unbroken, unmarred. The shade may change, but smoothly, gradually, so evenly that you can never draw a line, cannot even imagine a line, and say "Here the hue changes" or "Now one ends and the other begins". There is no end, there is no begin. There is only sky. There is only Air. Infinite.

Gaze into the Air, and see the clouds, always new, always fresh. There is so much that can be said about clouds! If everything ever written was all about clouds, it still would not be enough, would not be complete. Who has not stared at the clouds, seen the shapes, watched for the wonders, looked at the life that permeates the heavens? Everything is there, if you only look for it. And *only* if you look for it, for you put it there. Of itself, the cloud is only a random set of meaningless shapes. You put meaning into it, any meaning you wish, for there is no limit. There is no limit to the infinite.

Stare into the Fire. Leaping, dancing, cavorting flames, frantic, frolicing in a silent cacophony of heat and light, active, glowing, gleaming, eager, furious, exuberant, incandescent! Fire is silent. Air will roar when singed by the heat, Earth will crackle when scorched by the flame, Water will hiss when seared by the ember. But Fire is silent. All of its frenetic energy manifests in heat and light and motion. See moving pictures of faces, friends and fiends. See fantasy landscapes, mountains that meld into valleys in a flickering instant. See all that ever was, all that ever will be, all that you fear, all that you desire. See all that you want. See all. All is there, all of the time, all in a space so small and in a time so short. All in a campfire, or a candle, or a match. Everything is there, when you put it there. Infinite.

Peer into the Water. It reflects, ripples, distorts, and yet shows clearly whatever you see in it. What *you* see in it. It reflects *you*. See into the depths, put sights deeply within, and pull them out as deep insights. They are there, all of them, if you look. Listen to its voice. White noise, it is called. White, bright, revealing, pure. Random and meaningless, until you add the meaning. The meaning comes from you, from deep within you. Peer into the Water, and it will reflect you. All of you, everything that is in you. Infinite.

Earth, Air, Fire and Water. They are infinite, and they are nothing. They are utterly meaningless, until they are filled with meaning, with all of the infinite meaning there is. Be sure, it *is* there, but only because you put it there. We call it Imagination. You put it in there so that you can take it out. It is your way of telling yourself that which you really already know, just are not yet aware of. You not only are a part of the Universe, you are all of it.

You are infinite.

Earth

The Other People

Human people visit the Wilds to see the wildlife and view the forests. They recognize the Little People, the squirrels and birds, and the Wild People, the deer and elk and moose, and the Exotic People, the bison and bears. Many even acknowledge them as people. Inferior people, perhaps, but people none the less. They recognize the trees, and the types of trees. "Sure, those are evergreens, and those are, um, well, the other kind." Some can tell a pine from a pinyon from a fir, or a beech from an aspen. But very few would agree that the trees are people. Why, the very idea is fantastic!

No. "Fantastic" applies to the *other* people, the ones you can see in the rocks and waters and clouds and such. The people of Fantasy, of Imagination, of Make-Believe. The faerie and elves, the goblins and trolls; of course they do not exist, but...but they look so real, so *alive!* The happenstance shapes and freak coincidences that cause faces to peer down from clouds and peek out of cliffs. The pair of boles on the tree trunk that seem to be staring at you, very specifically at *you*. The sighing wind or singing brook that you would swear is calling your name. They are there, beyond any doubt, they do exist. Everyone has seen shapes in clouds, everyone except Charlie Brown. Some are so subtle that you can barely point them out, some so clear you would think someone carved them. And the more fertile your imagination, the more you will see. Are they, in some eldritch way, alive, aware? You know they are not, but are you certain? Would you be willing to, literally, bet your *life* on it?

Some you have to look for, hard. You really have to *want* to see them, for these do not want to be seen.

The Old Man, the moustache hiding the lips, long whiskers flowing below to cover cheeks and chin, gazes with his deep-set eyes across the vale.

An old troll squats and leans on one arm, knees in the air, and craggy head slumped on his chest.

A Green Goddess sprawls upon her stone throne, arms splayed to her sides, legs outstretshed, and chin hunched to her breast.

Trolls are common, for as we learn from the ancient legends, they cannot stand the sun, and turn to stone if caught in the light. Or maybe they are simply very patient, and do not mind sitting, unmoving, for a few thousand years. This one has sat still in his chair for so long, he is now half covered. His knees and shins protrude, along with head, shoulders and arms, and one hand on his breast, but his chest and his lap and the backs of his legs lie well-buried. Perhaps he is just being there, seeing the world. I like to do that myself. But not for so long.

Here is a river-troll. You do not see it in the picture, but he is watching a bridge, perhaps waiting for a billy goat Gruff. Trolls are noted for their long memories, little sense, and a deep regard for revenge.

The Other People may be fantastic and legendary, even mythical, but they are mortal. Some are very hard to kill, but they can die, they do die. The Frost Giants, the Fire Giants, even the great Stone Giants. This one is proof of the fact. How he . . . (yes, he is male; look between his legs). How he came to die, I cannot say, nor exactly when, but it was once upon a time, long, long ago. His head and arms and shoulders have been devoured by Time, and his legs are now buried to the knees, but still he stands, undaunted even in defeat. Or possibly not bright enough to realize he is dead.

Goblins abound in this shadowy world. They are also known as imps, fairies, sprites, and pixies. There may be differences between them, but I suspect no greater than the differences in human races. But they should not be confused with gnomes and leprechauns, which are of different species altogether. Also the Faerie, which are *not* cute little girls with transparent wings. Gnomes and leprechauns are little folk who pretty much just want to be left alone, and will not bother you if you do not bother them. Faerie will also leave you alone, unless the mood takes them to do otherwise. Best to have nothing to do with them. Goblins, on the other hand, are not good, and are not evil. I do not think they even understand the concepts of Good and Evil. Just Fun. All they really want to do is play, but that can be pretty bad, depending on what they consider to be fun. Like floods and wildfires.

The water sprites are my favorites. You can see them, if you look hard, but they will not photograph. Either the shutter speed is too slow, and all you get is a blur, or it is too fast, and you can only see tiny droplets. The air pixies, or winds, are also unrecordable, as they are completely invisible. You can only detect them by the results of their actions: Swaying trees, waving grass, ripples on ponds and such.. They have been known to play keep-away, dashing off with something in the hope that you will chase them. They are not too sure of what you may value, so they often run off with bits of litter, but sometimes they will snatch a hat or a letter or such. They often try for umbrellas, and think it a fine game to interfere with folding a map or sheet or tarpaulin. I have even seen them take off with an entire dome tent that the owner had erected but not staked down. The pixie would roll it fifty or a hundred feet, stop till the owner had almost reached it, then roll it again. I shamefully admit, I thought it was fun, too. It was not my tent.

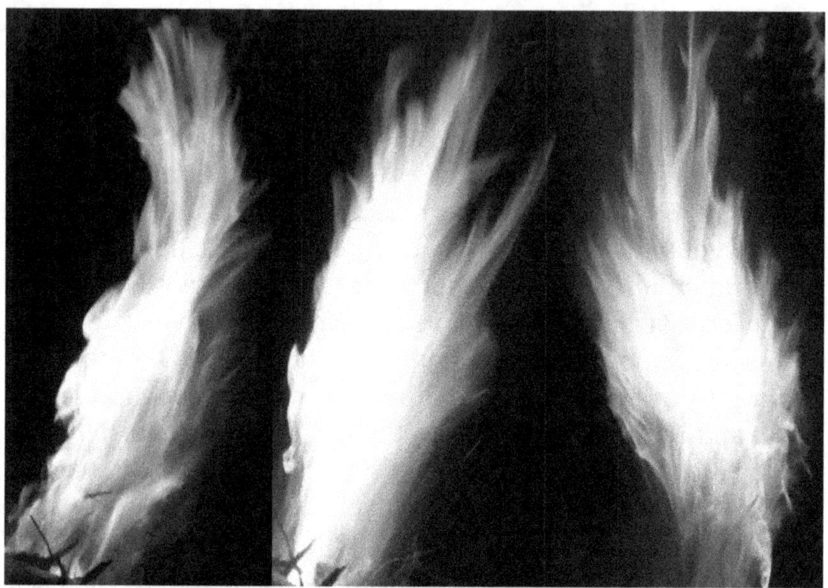

The imps in fire, though, those you can see. They are hard to photograph, very hard, and yet easy at the same time. They are so evanescent, they move so swiftly, that by the time the camera's shutter has clicked, the goblin is gone. But usually another has erupted, so you get an image of that one.

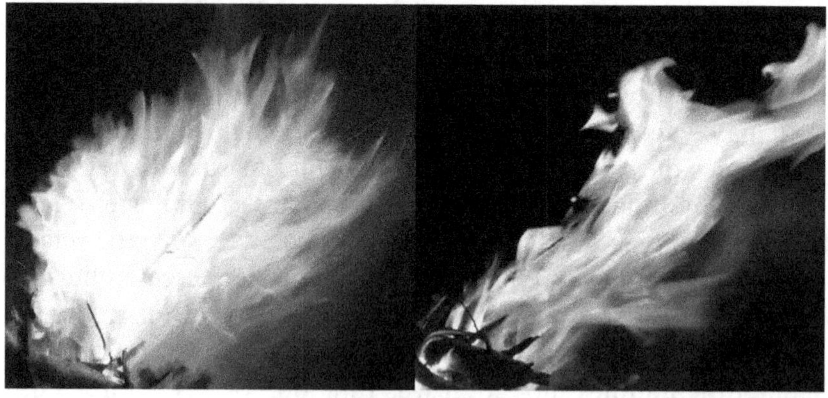

Spirits also abound in this world. I am a spirit (or soul, if you prefer) running a body as one would run a car. You are, too. I have known many animals, especially dogs, coyotes and ravens, who clearly were aware, and aware of being aware. That is the hallmark of a spirit. If we can inhabit these bodies, I see no reason we could not inhabit other things, animals, birds, brooks, even rocks. Okay, we could not get a rock to walk. I don't think we could. But maybe we could. Maybe we could shape the rock, cause it to take on a form we wanted. Many, probably most, of these shapes and images we see in rocks and clouds are purely imagination. Look at all of the fiction in our libraries, and you will agree, we can imagine some mighty strange things. But some are just too perfect to ascribe to random coincidence. For example:

Think about it.

Castles of Sand

Once upon a time, an ocean lay where I sit today. The animals and the birds have forgotten. Even the trees have forgotten. No, not forgotten, for they never knew. Their grandfather's grandfather's grandfathers did not know. Their long-long-ago ancestors, so long past they may well have been of a different species from the beings we know today, they are the ones who have forgotten. All have forgotten, it was so long ago, the streams, the rivers, the lakes, even the seas, all, all, except the rocks. They remember. They remember everything. They are God's diary, an essay on "What I Did on My Eon Vacation".

I sit in a gorge, a miniature canyon, not two feet wide at the base, and forty feet deep. The sides are of silt, the last traces of waters that eroded ancient hills, so long gone that these layered traces are the only remaining clue that they ever existed. Most of the silt is fairly coarse, and crumbles easily between finger and thumb, but some is very fine, so fine it has compacted under weight not great enough to compress the larger layers. This fine, weak mud has become the stronger, and draws lines across the face of the cliff, undercut by erosion. I judge the silt to be a sign of a time of drought, when long-starved rivers flowed weakly, and only the finest and lightest load was could be carried so far as this. But there were also floods, torrents, deluges, for I see seams of gravel and rock, some worn by long travel, and some as sharp as if broken from the bedrock only yesterday, some smaller than a fingernail, some bigger than my fist. What mighty masses of water must have moved across the land, to carry such a burden so great a distance!

I wonder what the rocks and sand and silt may think of this. Long, long ago, they were broken from the bedrock, and journeyed far to finally fall to the bed of the sea, there to rest and reform as new bedrock. But before they could complete their metamorphosis, the continent stirred and rolled in its slow sleep, and the seabed rose, exposing dark mud to the light of the sun, and rose, draining the last of the waters into the now distant sea, and rose, and rose, until the ancient silt stood more than a mile above its prior home. And now, once more, the silt must yield to the rain, and wash down, wash away, far away, beyond the horizon, for a thousand miles, and a thousand more, to return to the sea, to settle in its bed, to try again to compact and compress, solidify, harden back to bedrock before rising again. Are they frustrated at the interruption, or happy to be back at high altitude, glad of another opportunity to ride the water slides? Here is a flint, as long as my hand, which rode the waters and kept its form intact for so long. Now it lies half exposed, half buried, locked in the sheltering silt. But the water has reached it, and frozen in winter, and the flint has cracked, four long flakes that were once one. Does it lament its fate, and yearn for the safe years buried beneath the sea? Does it take the optimistic view, that smaller fragments will move faster, and return to the sea just that much sooner? They do not speak, they stand mute, dumb, as rocks.

Outside the canyon, I view the entire cliff. My little ravine is lost in its face, not half, not a quarter of its entire height. But the patterns remain, protruding ridges of incipient sandstone, serrating the surface , lying perpendicular to the vertical gullies that gouge the great wall. And far up, near the top, lies a ledge of sturdy rock white against the red-brown. It is solid, hard, strong. The ledge projects, resisting the rain as the rest of the cliff cannot, providing a shelter, armor against assault, for what the water cannot reach, it cannot erode. In places, the cap has cracked, and ice has broken holes to let the rain through. Here the rain has carved the cliff, and worked it into the shapes of fantasy, walls and towers, keeps and castles, shapes that should symbolize might and endurance. But only symbolize, for these castles are not only built upon sand, they are built of silt. They are mere illusions, the seeming of power, geological formations that are almost as ephemeral as the monuments built by Man. They will endure only so long as their solid pale capstones remain, the ridge, the white layer that is the opposite of a tombstone, for it preserves the body, not the memory.

In another sense, the ledge is a mausoleum. It must be composed of shells, the marble memorials of a great die-off, indicators of a massive poisoning of the whole inland sea. I search among the talus for a fallen fragment to prove the tale, and I discover one easily enough. But... it is another mystery: This is not calcium, it is volcanic ash, spewed from a gargantuan eruption, or from many at the same time. The layer is thick, four feet at least, and runs the length of the valley, both sides. But the mystery is, the ash is interleaved with layers of lava, paper thin layers, which could only have been made by lava so hot it ran like water. And thus the seabed must have been above water at that time. Yet the layering of silt continues unchanged above the volcano's signature. It had to have been a very shallow sea, and this was a mud flat, which refilled slowly, for there is no sign of erosion on any of its seams, no gullies, no breaks, not even a wave or a curl. Flat, straight, undisturbed. And yet, a few feet above, lies another stratum of lava and ash, the residuum of a second eruption, decades, maybe centuries after the first. Perhaps there were more. I cannot tell, for here the cliff ends, and the sky begins. Clearly, obviously, there were shifts and tremors and earthquakes when the continent began to move. Bedrock cracked, magma rose, fissures opened, and lava and ash spewed forth as the waters drained away. Then the land settled down, and the waters returned, for a short while, a breath of geologic time, before the land again moved, and the cracks reopened. The chaos repeated, the second layer lay on the mud. And then the land rose, and rose, and the ocean was no more. At least, not here. Clear. Obvious. But not necessarily true. There may have been a third layer, even a fourth. The answer does not lie here, for the rocks that knew do not lie here. If they ever did exist, they have departed, eroded and fled far away. They have been ground to silt, and washed to the sea, and in their reduction, have lost all memory of the forms they once wore. What is still here is remembered only by these rocks, and all others have forgotten. What was here, but is no more, is not remembered. It is forever forgotten, even by the rocks.

Even by the rocks.

Cloud Rocks

Rocks bear an inherent beauty, many inherent beauties It is only a matter of perceiving them. Every sculpture is nothing more than a shaped rock, physically altered to fit the sculptors mental image. Sometimes that image is purely arbitrary, and could be carved from a rock of any initial shape, but many are suggested to the artist by the original form. There is an old joke about the way to sculpt an elephant: All you have to do is cut away everything that does not look like an elephant. There is actually some truth to that jape. It depends on the artists ability to *see* the rock. I once found a fascinating rock, sort of a tear-drop shape in cross section, with both ends sheared off square. It was patterned with striations of dark red, red and pink, perpendicular to the flat ends. It looked exactly like a one hundred pound, well-marbled chuck roast. It was so clear, I became hungry. But then there was the mind-blind woman who, when I commented on the beauty of the rocks, shrugged and said they were only rocks, and walked on.

There is a mathematic called Fractal (short for Fractional Dimensions) Geometry. It can be used to generate images of seemingly random shapes such as mountain ranges. It has an interesting characteristic, in that any small section, when magnified, is indistinguishable from the larger picture. The details are different, but you cannot tell which is the original and which is the magnified segment.

Mountain ranges, as noted, display fractional geometry. So do the rocks which have split off from the mountains. There is a rock in front of me, about six feet wide and four feet high. In its broken face, I can see mountains. Here is one, a truncated volcanic cone, tilted twenty degrees to the left. Behind it is a more distant peak, roughly conical, less steep, and tilted 175 degrees to the right, almost upside down. Beside it is a third, but a sort of negative mountain, showing the typical shape, but instead of bas-relief, it is incised into the rock; it is the absence of rock that forms the mountain shape, as if air has become rock, and rock has become air. It is very surreal, and requires imagination and a long hard look to notice it, but the images are there, and are very precise. They could be photographed and extracted, and the image pasted over a photo of, say, Mount Shasta. If the task was performed with sufficient skill to hide the editing, one would accept it as an actual photo of a fourteen thousand foot mountain.

A change of viewpoint, not an alteration of physical position, but a shift in my consideration of what I am seeing, and I am looking down from twenty thousand feet at a broken and eroded high plateau. Here is a weathered mountain with a gully cut between two ridges. An abrupt cliff, a thousand feet high and almost sheer, plummets to a flat plain. Another ridge starts south, intersected by a third. A series of ravines lead down, down, and an alluvial fan spreads south. The entire landscape is incredibly detailed, fractally detailed just as far as I can perceive.

Another change of viewpoint reveals the face of the Nome King from the movie *Return To Oz*, with nose, eyes, mouth, sardonic grin. And it melts into a bear, the bridge of the nose forming a foreleg, the eyebrow becoming the underside of the neck, a black nose and bared teeth. It is like watching for pictures and shapes in clouds, except that the it is the clouds themselves that change, to melt into new shapes. The rock does not change, except for minutely shifting shadows as the sun courses across the sky, subtle changes revealing differing textures, sudden reflections, evanescent colors. The images in the rock do not themselves change, but drift only with your imagination, and can be resummoned at will. You can search for a particular image to see if it is there, or you can see what is there and let it make the image. It is better than a movie; it is a natural motion picture. The longer you look, the more you see. You become intimate with the rock. You gaze into it, and it gazes back at you. You come to *know* that rock, and it becomes your friend.

I wonder, what does it see in me?

Images

I headed east from Castle Rock, planning to do something over three hundred miles to the green Colorado mountains. I had a nice tailwind, which, unbeknownst to me, grew stronger and stronger as the day progressed. Aside from a few gusts when I passed through canyons, it was really quite pleasant. Then I turned south, and the tailwind revealed its true force. I did not say "Oh, dear!" I cannot tell you what I did say. Not if I intend to publish this. I put up with it as far as Arches National Park, where I decided to stop for the night, and finish the passage early tomorrow, before the wind rose. It being mid-September, most of the tourists were back in the cities, at work and at school. Even so, at the park entrance was the Dreaded Sign: Campground Full. On a Wednesday. Fortunately there are a dozen or so BLM campgrounds east of Moab, so I headed off to find a site. I did not much care about quality, as it was just a place to sleep for one night. The first one was full. So was the second. And the third. The fourth had just one site open, so in about five minutes, it was also full. Fifteen minutes later a fellow biker came from the other direction, and reported that all of the campgrounds upriver were also full. On Wednesday. In the off-season. So I offered to share my site. Bikers do that.

It is not a bad campground. A couple of sites have shade. Not mine. Just some scrub, not five feet tall. It is far enough from the highway that I need not fear getting run over. Why, it is almost twice as far as I can spit! Not too hot, mid-eighties, and tonight should be mid-forties. No water, trash, firewood. But it is not crowded or cramped; it has room, with a view.

Just north, two or three times as far away as the highway, lies the Colorado River. The north bank is Arches National Park. Rising right from the river is a talus slope, forty-five degrees, well over a hundred feet high, and from that, at least as tall, a craggy, broken, vertical cliff of red stone. And the south bank is much the same, only having a flat area wide enough for the campground and then the highway, then the talus, worn red rocks standing in crumbled gravel and shattered stone, long ago, or maybe just this morning, fallen from the cracking cliffs. At one point stand several spires, ten times as tall as their bases are broad. One of them, perhaps twenty feet wide, stands next to the parent bluff, set apart by a narrow crevice only two to four feet wide. How could this come to be? What forces could carve this miniscule gap, but leave a narrow needle beside it? It is not a freak, not at all unusual, for I have seen literally hundreds of similar stones scattered throughout the Southwest. There are many towns whose names reflect this, Spires and Needles and such. They are common. If the strata had been tilted to the vertical, then softer seams could erode away. I have seen that; two natural walls, each a foot wide, ten feet apart, and running hundreds of feet up the hillside, separated by a gap with nothing but gravel remaining, looking for all the world like a medieval curtain-wall, faced inside and out with dressed stone, and filled between with rubble. But every stratum here is flat, horizontal, not tilted at all. I can guess, but I do not know. That is okay. The world should have some mysteries.

The horizontal layers and the vertical ridges catch the light in different ways at different times of day. Sometimes they show shadows, emphasizing their presence and dramatizing the differences in the textures of the rock. One cliff appears almost perfectly smooth in early morning or late afternoon sun, but near noon displays ledges and footholds, as pocked and scarred as a banana republic's execution wall. Nearby, another section comprises nothing but ragged teeth, like a carpenter's rasp writ large, but as day progresses, the shadows dwindle to nothing at noon, and the face seems almost smooth, only a bit irregular.

And the faces, why, there are faces everywhere. They are easy to spot. Simply look for a horizontal line with a vertical beneath it, a "T". There you have the brow of the eyes and the bridge of the nose. Often there is a ledge below to serve as lips, and perhaps a knob, the chin. And as the shadows change, so do the faces. Some show themselves only at noon. There is

one to the East, glowering, angry in early afternoon, gloomy and sad at sunset. But in the morning, it is not there at all, though if you know him already, you can see where he will be. And rarely, very rarely, there is a complete face, with all features present, all in proportion, such as Monkey Falls, or the young Goblin of Castle Rock, clearer and even more obvious than

New Hampshire's late Old Man of the Mountain. Humanoid faces are easy to find, for they are our favorite pattern, and our imaginations will seek them in all things. But there are animals as well, horses and bison, wolves, eagles, whales, and trees, tall pines and spreading oaks, conical spruce, whatever you want to see. But you must *want* to see them. They are shy, and will not come out to play with just anyone.

And there are castles and ships, and walls and chairs, breasts and phalluses, hands raised in gestures of greeting or warning or insult. Everything is there, reflected in rock, for the source is, like beauty, in the eye of the beholder. There are exceptions, such as the Castle Rock Gnome, who could not have been carved more clearly by Michaelangelo himself. But no dog will note the stone hand gesturing "OK", though he may be momentarily confused by a palm-forward hand saying *stay!*

The clouds are more expressive, for they are constantly changing, and they show more shapes, but you must be quick, for in a few seconds, the image may be gone, or may become something else. But you also must look, consciously look, for the images are imaginary, and thus you must also think. Rocks are better, for though they say less, what they show is more weighty, less transient. The flighty clouds babble, with little substance; the solid rocks orate, in slow and stately measured sentences. They give you time to ponder, to look more deeply, and it is in the depth, never on the surface, that you find the true insights.

Ooh, look at the rocks!

Seeing It All

Small clouds scattered across the sky spread their shadows upon the land, now in light, now in shade, over and over, patternless, and of little consequence save to sun-bathers and shade-seekers. And to photographers, both those with camera machines and those with living eyes and lucid minds. For the photographs made by the machine are weak and flat things, even the motion pictures. They record a small insipid image that only hints at the real scene. They lack depth, both physical and metaphysical. They lack the scale, the sheer size; is that rock ten feet tall, or a hundred? They lack the context, the setting, the surroundings, everything not in the narrow frame. They lack the *world*. And they lack life. Even the great IMAX images, breathtaking as they can be, pale and dwindle next to the thing itself. They capture a deer, the grace, the swiftness, and the imprisoned image can be beautiful indeed. But the live deer twenty feet from you emanates a *presence*, a *thereness*, life and mind and reality that no one has ever succeeded in capturing, except in live memory. It is detected by the being, it communicates with the mind, it impresses itself in ways that words cannot describe, only approximate. Life *knows* when it is in the presence of life. Pictures, however detailed, contain no life.

It is much the same with landscapes, especially waterfalls and mountains and cliffs. I am sitting in the presence of a cliff hundreds of feet high, deeply carved over many millenia by the

Shoshone River. Half of the cliff is clothed by verdant conifers in scattered stripes. The rest is rock, bare rock, jagged rock, cracked and striated, slowly eroded by water and wind and expanding ice, torn into ridges and rifts, into spires and pinnacles and promontories. Here a massive monolith arrogantly projects perpendicular to the cliff face, half as long as it is high, and seven times as high as it is thick, a rough-cut slab of stone arrogantly impacting itself upon the clouds.

There a series of spines silhouette against sky, dull, dark, matted green-brown. Down below them run ridges, sloping swiftly toward the river, breaking abruptly half-way down, and terminating in torn knobs of rugged rough rock, fractured and crumbling, threatening to dive into the waters far below. All is dark pastels, wide impressionist brush strokes emphasizing form over detail.

And then the shadow passes, and the bright sun strikes. Instantly the view is transformed into a mass of detail, tiny sharp shadows delineating every crack and crevice, exposing every rock and ridge, emphasizing the talus fallen to the cliff, desperately clinging to ledge and slope, terrified of the waiting abyss below. The uniform brown is gone, revealed as tan and beige and red and yellow and orange, every imaginable shade and hue. The rock is no longer smooth. Now it is pocked and stippled and carved and scratched, lines, hollows and dimples deep and shallow. Razor-sharp ridges reveal gouges and gullies previously invisible under uniform shadow. And the cloud-shadow returns, fingers of darkness smoothing away all detail and design, leaving a bland brown mass where once was a vision so intricate that could gaze on it in wonder for hours, constantly discovering infinite new delights. Then the shadow moves on, and the detail is re-engraved, just as before, but subtly different, for the angle of the sun has changed, slightly, ever so slightly. If the light were constant, one might become aware of the change after an hour, or half an hour, for the change is so smooth and so slow that one must remember, *this* shadow was not there, and *that* one was not so wide. But with the irregularity of the light, the coming and going, the hiding and revealing, the changes stand out. The strange shadow that looks like a tree is there no longer. The crack that looked like a flake about to fall is seen to be simply a scratch in the side of solid stone. The hillside is seen in a gargantuan strobe, with intervals as long as the mountain is high. For this is the scale of the wide world, and our tiny bodies are less to it than the smallest of gnats is to us, and far less annoying.

And this is what no picture can capture, a scale so great that people cannot grasp it. I know, intellectually, that scarp is five hundred feet higher than I, and near to half a mile away. I know it is huge. I know it is massive. I imagine what it would be like to stand at its base, and I am awed. Then I cross the river, and painfully find a passage, and after hours of travail, achieve my goal, and actually stand at the base, and ... there are no words, not adequate to the task. The rock rises forever, ten, twenty, fifty times beyond what it soared in my feeble attempt at imaginings. The closest I can come to expressing the holy grandeur is to note that this one brief sight was well worth the hours of struggle to make it possible.

And now the sun is setting, ducking under the clustering clouds. The light loses the yellow, and burns a hot orange and red. The new color rebounds from the mountain, and once again everything changes. The shapes seem the same, but the contrasts are inconstant, the textures transformed, rough rock now seeming fibrous and fluffy, solids turning soft, threatening to melt, flow, ooze down the hill.

I read this over, and look at the rocks. I have fallen so far short of reality. I look at pictures taken of the hill, and they fall even further short of my words. But if you only feel tempted, then I have succeeded. If you feel the urge, give in to it. Follow the Shoshone towards Yellowstone. There are many campgrounds, and almost all have a similar view. Pick a site. Sit down and stare at the cliffs till they stare back at you. See them in their many gaudy garbs of light and darkness. A mere glance is of no value; but if you *can* just glance and look away, then you are missing something inside. If so, do not despair. Gaze upon the grandeur, and that missing something will grow in you, and on you. Look, *really* look, and see what is there, see it as much as you are able. If for whatever reason you cannot visit the Shoshone, there are many, a great many, other, similar, even better opportunities. Find one. See it. Grow into it. It will reward you, many times over. And you will never be the same again.

Air

The Hilltop

On a quiet hilltop in Northern New Mexico, a few hours after dawn. There is not a trace of cloud, and the air is cool, and calm. The hill is crowned with a blend of pines and firs and cedars, tall ones, mature, lording over a layer of young trees, who look down upon the saplings. The saplings all sprouted during the last ten years. The young ones are all sixty or seventy years, and the patriarchs, past a century and a half. Probably fires sweep the hills once or twice every human lifetime and youth is, as always, sacrificed to the war. The seedling boom follows, and the first of them survive the next hostilities, but not the youngest. Now that I look, I see several patriarchs well into their second or third century, yet no taller than the succeeding generation. They grow thicker each year, but it seems that once they attain a certain height, they grow no taller. Not on this hill. Is it shallow soil? Do the midgets survive while the giants lose their footing? I do not see their bones, but they may have melted into the hill. Perhaps it is wind, or lack of it. With no wind to sway the trees, it would be hard for them to pump water to the topmost twigs.

Hilltops are not usually calm, but this one is. A random zephyr from time to time is all I have felt, barely enough to bend the grass and twinkle the fir needles. The trees do not sway, their limbs do not toss. And yet I do hear the wind, a distant exhalation, an "Ahh!" of pleasure as the treetops tickle the belly of the air. Each wind is alive, a creature of the skies as each fish is a citizen of the seas. Each breeze is a baby, each gust a child of the aerial family. Many clans and tribes of the airborne hordes sweep along overhead, invisible, undetected, unknown. How many hundreds or thousands of millions of faeries fly far above us every day, hour, minute? How many watch me as I watch them back? Do they see me as I see them, not by vision but by knowing they are there? The young ones slide on the slopes of the hills, giggling and cheering with breathy voices, north and south and all around. But not here, not on this hill. A taboo ground? A holy place? Or just, not as much fun as that hill over there?

And then it comes, a whisper, a "Shush!", a "Whhy-y-y?", a warning "Aahhh!" The zephyr leaps, it ruffles my hair, the small trees tremble and the topmost treetops sway a foot, two, four, eight feet and more and - - - a sudden stillness settles in the air. All motion stops in a swift silence, the residual sway damping down and diminishing to nothing. A second surge that touches the tallest tops, but only the sound and sight reaches me. Again it is calm, but the sounds remain, from east and west and every bound.

For an hour, there was nothing save a wandering wisp, a tremble of grass, a flicker of twig. Then an hour of calm and surge, four, maybe five times, random and rare. Now the sun is high, the hill grows warm. The breeze becomes steady. Not strong, but enough to maintain a constant motion in the flowers and grass, balmy, not cool, not warm. Branches wiggle and twist, but trunks remain stable. A steady sussurus, too slight for a hiss, an eternal sigh broken only by the buzz of a questing bee. The shade slips away and hides beneath the trees. The rocks brighten and warm, remembering their molten birth so long, long ago. The rising heat raises the wind, and the spread branches twist the boles. The breezes have grown, they have graduated from grasses and now are the movers and shakers of trees, the exuberant youths changing the world. Now the trees toss, and dance in a dignified pavane, slow and solemn, and pompous and proud. And yet, as stolid as they are, aloof and independent, they are, whether they will or not, dancing to the wind's tune, the song of the faerie, of the spirits of the air. But how long does a wind live? The jet stream is nearly immortal; the first puffs of dawn last mere seconds. Gust-slinger winds may order the trees to dance, but they soon will pass, and the orderly trees will remain, tranquil, in peace. Rooted in earth and water, fearing only the fire, the trees let the wind pass away, as they always have, always do, and always will. The trees stand tall in the midday sun, on the quiet hilltop in the center of the universe, in the middle of eternity, in the midst of life. And they are content.

Speaking of Wind

Wind has a voice, and the voice speaks words, and the words have meaning. The meaning is nothing deep, nothing wise. At least, no meaning that I have ever understood. The wind is a child who is just learning to speak. On an outing with the parents, the child will point and say "Dog!" The meaning is not "big dog" or "nice dog", or even "look at the dog"; only "dog", and nothing more. So it is with the wind. It blows through a pine and makes a distinctive whisper. In no other tree does it make that precise sound, only in the pine. The wind is saying "Pine!" The meaning of that whisper is "pine". There are subtle nuances heard from bigger, older winds with larger vocabularies: Big pine, small pine, Lodgepole Pine, Ponderosa. It is still the same basic word, "pine". There is another word, closely related, meaning "fir", and another for "spruce". Very similar, but different, the same as is the case with all single-syllable words beginning with "s". If you do not *listen*, they sound pretty much the same, as to an ancient Greek, who heard in foreign languages only "bar-bar, bar-bar" (and hence we get the word "barbarian").

For other woods there are other words, as distinctive as our words "pine" and "aspen" and "oak". Where "pine" is a whisper, "aspen" is almost a patter, a softly slurred tapping, with barely a hint of a cricket's chirp. Listen to recordings of wind in pines and wind in aspens, and you can clearly hear the difference, as different as the sounds of "s" and "ch". The words for "oak" and "maple" carry a click, almost, sharper in the oak, softer in the maple. "Tall grass" is a gentle rasp, like a violin bow sliding on the edge of a table, with just a touch of rattle. And there is another word, a hiss with no sibilance, a whistle with no tune, which means "snag", a dead tree with leafless branches.

A beginner can learn the words in mono-cultures, woods with only one type of tree. A trained ear can pick them out in a mixed forest. When you have become fairly fluent in Windish you can learn more words. It is much like German, in that complex words are formed by stringing together many smaller words, except that in Windish, all of the smaller words are pronounced simultaneously. For example, the words for pine, oak and aspen, snag and grass, with all of the "tall tree" and "short tree" variations thrown in, and all spoken at once, is the word for "forest". Rather, it is *a* word for forest, for each such word labels and describes a specific part of a particular forest. It is the name of those acres as well as a label, and a pretty complete description of them. Much like Entish, but faster. If you listened hard enough, and long enough, in many different places, you could identify locations by nothing more than the sound. The wind would tell you where you are. But I do not recommend trying. I suspect that "long enough" would be several human lifetimes.

This is another of Nature's pranks, a parable, perhaps to teach us humility. A wind, which has such a brief lifespan, minutes, hours, perhaps a week (except, of course, the jet streams and trade winds), knows almost from birth the airy language, and learns it swiftly, learns it like, well, like the wind. And we, the clever, intelligent, "wise man", cannot possibly learn more then a pidgen version.

I wonder what the jet stream knows.

Gusts

In a way, this is the worst wind I have ever known. Not the strongest, nor the most prolonged. That was a hurricane in the Caribbean. For that matter, I have known swifter winds in the mountains of Wyoming, and in the flat low desert of Arizona. Faster sustained winds. More powerful gusts, too. This wind is fairly strong, probably thirty knots when steady, and gusty, sixty and seventy knots at its peaks. I have known worse. But what I have not experienced before is the intensity. Not raw power, for the gusts are not the strongest, but there are three times as much of them. The wind is extremely erratic, three quarters gusts, and only one quarter steady wind, or lulls. Plastic dome tents are designed to flatten when the wind is too strong. Anything over thirty-five or so, and their fiberglass rods bend and flex and the tent lies down, a reed letting the wind pass over. When the gust subsides, the rods reassert themselves, and the tent stands back up. If I was in a dome tent today, the rods would be heating up and probably starting to splinter from the frequent repetition, flex and straighten, flex and straighten, over and over and over. That is, assuming the fabric had not shredded.

But I have a stout canvas tent, a tent designed to handle strong wind and heavy gusts, and redesigned to cope with points I overlooked before. Every seam is doubled. Every stress point is reinforced. The join of walls and roof are lined with 3/8" manila rope, so most of the stress is taken by rope, not cloth. The main tentpoles are steel, and are paired, two poles lashed together for double strength. The guys are also doubled at each corner, manila ropes set ninety degrees apart, and held by nine-inch steel spikes. This tent could not endure a hurricane or a tornado, but this wind? I have full confidence in it. Even so, I cannot simply sit complacently and neglect the weather. It is the gusting, you see. Repeated stress and slack, a very, very slow vibration, pulls on the guy ropes, then releases them, over and over. Each pull slacks the rope a tiny fraction of an inch, a hundredth or less. After a few hours, there are a couple of inches of extra slack, so I must make a round and tauten them back where they belong. No problem there.

There are a few problems, minor ones. One of the tent curtains worked loose, and its rope caught on a large splinter. The gusts put a strain on the fabric which it had never been intended to endure, and now the curtain is ripped halfway across. It is no hazard to the tent, and does not diminish the shelter, but it will require a couple of hours of work to mend it and alter it so such damage does not recur; I will have to make the same changes to the other curtain. And there is the effect of the wind on cooking. Obviously, there is no chance of a campfire. There is not a possibility the fire may be scattered and ignite another wildfire; there is utter certainty. I doubt even a city-dweller would consider a campfire today. The wind is even too much to allow use of a gasoline stove, for it would snatch the heat away from the pot, if it did not snuff the flame altogether. Fortunately, I am residing at a campsite that has electricity available, so I can still have a hot meal. Of course, the wind has apparantly downed a power-line, so the power is off at the moment. But my problems are small, trivial, really.

You may have caught my mention of *another* wildfire. No, I have never started one myself. But two days ago, the Forest Service, taking advantage of cool weather, moderate fire hazard, and a prediction of only light winds, did a controlled burn a few miles from here. They finished their little burn successfully, but even a small managed fire requires a few days to be completely extinguished. Larger logs and stumps can quietly burn for days, and deep duff can conceal red sparks silently smouldering, hidden, smokeless, barely gasping for air. A good strong wind can resurrect a seemingly dead fire. Alas, the weather forecast was not entirely accurate. This wind came along, and the controlled burn blew up. It is now completely out of control. The sky to the South is thick, solid smoke. The freeway fifteen miles to the East is closed because of zero visibility. And there is a town five miles further on.

I am safe, so long as the wind remains westerly. But should it back to the South, my camp will lie directly in its path. If the fire runs at thirty miles per hour (and with this wind, it very well could), it might be here in ten minutes. Essential gear is packed on the bike. The rest is in a clearing where it is unlikely to burn. I am sleeping fully clothed tonight. If the wind shifts, I am outta here!

Colors of the Air

The night sky is only black when seen by itself, over the deep ocean, far from land, beyond the reach of the loom of lighted cities. Even then, it is not fully black, but only seems so by contrast with the splendor of the stars. In a full overcast of unbroken cloud, far from any man-made lights, only then will the heavens lie black above us. Even in the deep desert on the darkest night, starlight on the sands reflects back to soften the shadow, to brighten the sky by an infinitesimal amount. The horizon is visible, jagged with distant mountains, not subtle, but sharp and distinct. The astronauts describe a sky so full of stars that it almost seems white. The vast majority of stars visible from Earth are too dim to be discerned through the atmosphere. The air shatters and scatters the light, and just as frosted glass turns a view into a uniform off-white, so does the air turn the black of space into a deep gray.

It begins in the East. The black fades or the mountains deepen; it is hard to say which, but the distinction is greater. It is almost as if the sky was growing lighter. Then it is sure. It is grey. Greyness rises slowly, but swiftly extends north and south, a dollop of pale light spilled in the East and flowing around the horizon, delineating the dome, separating the sky, bearing the black away from the Earth. Light grows, deep grey, true grey, pale grey, infinite gradations never named. It strains against the black, strains until the light breaks. Palest pink appears, a blush, not of shame, but of life. It brightens to red, to orange, to yellow, encircling the whole horizon, a golden ring wedding the Earth and the Sky. The Sun appears,

Son of the Dawn, resplendent, glorious. The golden ring absorbs the orange, the red, the yellow, the blue, and a band of glowing white defines the horizon, easing through every possible degree of blue to the bright deepness of the zenith. All of the colors of the air, the full spectrum, every basic hue.

Except one. For there is no green, not a single trace or even hint of green.

Green is not a color of the air. It belongs to the land, to Life. It is foreign to the sky, which is allowed to look upon green, but only look. The fabled Green Flash is not of the sky, but of the sun, and it is fleeting, and reticent. Twice I have seen it, in the Caribbean. It is nothing like the Disney fantasy, no flare, no spectacle, no sound. When the sun is setting, at the last possible instant, when only the slightest sliver of sun remains, if the air conditions are just exactly right, that tiniest trace of sun turns green, bright green, glowing green, greener even than Ireland. For only an instant, not half of a second, a flash, and it is gone. It is not of the sky. It is not of the sea.

Green belongs to Life. Water, ponds, the sea, they can be green, but it is Life that colors them, not the water. The rainbow bears green, but while it is in the air, it is not of the air; it is Light showing off its fancy pretties. Rocks will sometimes show a small section of green, rarely, a sort of grace note in the thing least known for grace. What poet ever wrote of "graceful granite"? Green belongs to life. In the air, it means Death. I have seen it, in Oklahoma. I was five, perhaps six. The family was gathered in the yard, watching the sky, watching the clouds, the swirling, twisting tail forming and dissolving, reaching tentatively toward the land, pulling back, forming again, drifting south. It was miles away when, with sudden decisiveness, it leaped to the ground, swift as a snake, roaring, raucous, thunderous, trampling, tearing, embodiment of devastation, Angel of Death, Finger of God . . . And through it all, the sky was Green. Dark green, grey-green, the color of corruption, of decay, of rot, a putrid, pestilent, gangrenous green you could almost smell, the color, the sound, the smell of Death.

Fascinating, not frightening, to a boy of five, who does not yet understand that he can and will die, for it fled to the South, away, not here.

Here it is color, the forest is still, the air barely stirs. The Sun is only inches above the hills, shining through trees, lighting the leaves with a yellowish loom. All of the green is in the leaves, in grass and bush and sapling and tree. The sky is blue, and yellow and white. The last rays of red and orange dart from the Sun. There are the colors of peace, and of life, and the colors of the air.

Fire

Bright Love

It is cold this morning. Not too cold. Still a couple of degrees above freezing. Pleasantly cold. I have not even donned my long underwear. I am comfortable, because I have a young friend to keep me warm. She is bright and cheerful, active, quick. I love her very much, for along with keeping me warm and cooking my meals, she makes me think, she ignites my imagination, she hints of marvels never seen in the mundane world, she speaks of magic and dreams, and sheds light upon my world and my wonder. And all she asks of me is that I feed her. If I do not feed her, she turns sullen and ashen and cold. But later, when I bring her more sustenance, and tickle her, she forgives me and comes back, as bright and cheerful as ever, for she has no memory.

She lies before me now, hot, bright, glowing. I prod her, stir her coals, add a few more sticks, and the flames respond, leaping aloft. Here, sitting beside her, there is no cold, there is no darkness.

What a wonder is fire! All she asks is wood and wind, a little fuel, a breath of air. She is born as the tiniest of sparks, so small one would not even feel her upon the skin, but should she land upon tinder, the dust of wood or fungus or charcoaled leaves or linen, she will feed and grow, enough to set a flame in pine needles or shredded bark, to grow and light twigs and sticks and branches and logs, even, if not carefully restrained, entire forests! She is clean, clearer than a mountain stream, and when she has finished and passed away, even her white and powdered bones will mix with water and wash away the most stubborn grease and grime. But if interrupted, if stopped and quenched before her work is done, she will blacken and befoul all that touches her remains. She will clean and purify a forest, reducing the rotting carcasses of dead trees and discarded branches to nutritious ash, fertilizer for the living, pap for the new generation. But should man intervene, and keep her from her task, the fire will eventually rise in all her anger, and rage through the woods with such ferocity that nothing will survive, nothing in her reach. Beware, arrogant humans! Honor the Fire, and interfere with her at your own risk!

Fire is fragrant, and will perfume the air with many of the sweetest scents, the aromas of woodsmoke. There are many, and few are foul. The smoke of apple, and maple, and hickory, and mesquite, each tastes as sweet as it smells, and we use it to flavor our foods. Spruce, pine and juniper smell like camping and living outdoors. The smallest wisp is sufficient to set loose the imagination, to carry the mind away on a spiritual vacation. But do not grow greedy! Take smoke in moderation, for too much, a very small too much, will choke you and blind you and drive you away, reeling and gasping. And even worse, when the Wildfire rages, she may send before her writhing and roiling coils of smoke, thick, dense, hot, choking clouds that will drive the air from your lungs and deprive you of any more, crushing and hammering you to the ground, where you will lie, dead or helpless, till the fire arrives to scorch your bones. Again, be wary, and respect the fire! She has no pity, she knows no mercy, she will sear you and kill you, and neither know nor care. She will not even laugh.

And yet fire is a friend. She is a companion for the lonely, and a comforter for the cold. She guides the lost to safety, and wards off the wild beast. She is a tool. She melts our metals, hardens our pots, disposes of debris. And she is a servant, who cooks our food and lights our paths and our homes at night. But do not trust her! No, never trust a fire. She is loyal under duress, only so long as she is kept confined and watched, strictly watched. A woman scorned has no fury like a fire neglected, for then she will char your food and destroy your home, and she will warm you to death!

You do not need to worship fire, though many have done so, and some still do. You should acknowledge her, for if fire should cease to be, and never burn again, most people would die, and every civilization would fall and vanish into myth. But you must respect her, and be ever wary, for if you do not, she will kill you, one way or another. You can, if you wish, love her. I certainly do. She gives me so much. If I had no fire, I would be cold right now, or still in my sleeping bag, missing the morning till the sun came up. My motorcycle would not move, and I would have to abandon two-thirds of my gear, or be condemned to stay here, never to roam again. Food would have so much less flavor, and I would never again taste fried chicken or bread. Well, perhaps I could make do with the lightning. An electric bike, electric heater and stove. It could be done. But life would be much harder, much less convenient. And there would be no flames.

The Middle Eastern religions speak of a Hell of never-ending fire. My ancestors, the Scandinavians, knew a Hell of eternal ice. That speaks to me, for a place that could never know fire would surely be Hell.

Smoke Billow

The morning is cold, and the chill of the air is biting after the warmth of the sleeping bag. Last night, the fire was banked, the crimson coals covered with ash, in the hope they would survive till dawn. A stir with a stick proves their success, exposing their nearly starved and suffocated glow to the re-invigorating air. A few handfuls of dry leaves, a peck of tiny twigs and kindling, then a double dose of small branches and a log or two hide the gleam. In a very few seconds, wisps arise, thin tendrils of white, dry mists, ghosts escaping the pile of forest trash. The thin puffs expand and grow and multiply to form a column of smoke, rising at an angle to the pine branches above. The column thickens and darkens, a noxious cloud, a pillar almost solid, roiling, billowing, writhing into the air. A few warning crackles and pops issue from the fire pit, and with an instant suddenness and a muffled roar, the entire pyre bursts into light and flame, and the smoke stream is cut off as abruptly and sharply as a rope is sliced short by a well-honed knife. The column continues to billow and drift away, but with no more smoke to renew it, soon vanishes in the trees, leaving no trace to show it once had been, nothing except a lingering aroma.

The campfire is welcome warmth in the often bitter chill of a frosty morning. It is also a cheerful, relaxing glow on the tired faces of friends, worn and weary from a day in the woods, hiking or fishing or hunting, boating or swimming, whatever one does in the free and open Wilds. It is the beginning and the end, the alpha and omega, the very symbol of camping. The heat and the glow are remembered and treasured. But what is scorned or derided, if not neglected entirely, is the smoke.

Smoke is usually the sign of the duffer, the cheechalko, the tenderfoot. He uses green wood, or not enough, and creates choking clouds that chase him about, always enfolding him wherever he may sit, or so he will swear. But smoke is not all bad. It is the drumroll, the fanfare, that announces the newly kindled fire has well and truly caught. It is the confirmation that the old fire has not died, that fresh wood has rejuvenated it, and that it will very soon burst forth into a brilliant blaze.

Smoke is not always a thing shameful or embarassing, for no fire is truly, completely free of smoke. No wood fire, at least. At its birth and its death, the plume will be present. When the fire falters, and new wood is added, the fresh fuel flung upon the flames will char and hiss, and wisps of smoke will arise, often consumed by the existing flames, before the new sticks burst into blaze. Some smoke is inevitable, always. A cookfire kept at the correct temperature will often smoke, for a smokeless fire is hotter, and too much heat will blacken your bread, or burn the outside of your meat while leaving the center cold and raw. The moderate fire will smoke, a little, at least.

Smoke is even desireable, at certain times. A good thin smudge, not quite enough to tear the eyes or claw at the throat, will drive off the mosquitos and the no-see-ums, bringing comfort and surcease to the tortured woodsman. Smoke will scent the air with an aroma that years, even decades later will trigger nostalgia and fond memories of an otherwise forgotten vacation in the woods, of a childhood two-week respite from the baking concrete and asphalt jungle. Smoke will flavor the food we cook within it; the very best campfire bread must be exposed to the flames, licked by the smoke, absorbing the smell as flavor.

Smoke is also a visual experience. Have you ever watched the smoke? Not just seen it, not merely noted its presence, but *watched* it, as you would watch a movie, or stare at a cloud? The same phantasms and figures that lurk in clouds and rocks also dwell in the smoke, the long-eared bunnies and the surging schooners, the knights and dragons, and especially the faces. The same images, exactly the same, for the smoke cloud and the rain cloud are brother and sister, tiny particles, one of water, one of carbon, the basics of life, borne in the air, billows and fringes and fluffs, twisted and tossed, molded and shaped by invisible currents and eddies. The only real difference is that the smoke is so much faster, and its moving pictures are instantaneous, there to be seen, and gone in the instant of recognition, metamorphosed into an image unrelated in any way. Thus the face becomes a tree then a squirrel then a mountain, all in less time than it takes to name them. But as the column of smoke rises and thickens, it cools and slows, and the more the smoke cloud becomes like the rain cloud, so do the images slow and, in the end, become identical.

Pay attention to the smoke. It is as essential and worthy a part of the campfire as the warmth and the light. Rarely is fire created solely for the smoke. In fact the smoke is usually an unwanted and unneeded side affect. But it can be of value, if you wish it to be so. Great value. It can flavor and preserve food. Many lost or injured travelers have summoned aid with a smoky fire. Remember, the path to the Promised Land was marked by a pillar of smoke.

And it sure can be purty.

Burn, Baby, Burn

A few days ago, as I was heading north across the Mogollen Rim, I passed west of a wildfire. It was too far away to see, as I was passing through a forest of tall ponderosa pine, and was downwind, so I could see and smell no smoke. If it was not for the signs warning of fire-fighting vehicles and possible smoke, I would not have known that the Coconino National Forest was aflame. But after some thirty miles of northing, I could see, far off to the right, thick, white smoke. The wind was moderate, maybe fifteen miles per hour, so I figured the Forest Service teams had a fair chance of containing the blaze. But only fair, for conditions were *very* dry, extreme, in fact. There had been no rain since August, eight months ago. A freak turn of the jet stream this past winter had cut the country in two; all of the weather, all of the snow and rain, had fallen in the North and East. I mean *all* of it. Utah and Colorado had no snow pack; Arizona was as arid as Hollywood would portray. New Mexico was entirely, every square inch, under extreme fire danger. The Red Flag was flying over an entire state, and half of two others.

Fortunately, my destination lay in the midst of a desert plain. Dry, yes. Highly flammable, of course. But it just did not bear enough vegetation to present a significant hazard. If the plain did catch fire, the flames would probably sweep right past the campground, with perhaps a spot fire here or there that would be simple to stamp out. At worst, a quick backfire just before the blaze arrived would bring it to a crackling halt. But there were miles of similar plain between me and the fire, and an Interstate Highway as well.

Shortly after I arrived, the wind picked up. Soon it was blowing at thirty to forty miles per hour, and gusting to fifty. Well, that precluded any use of backfire, but the conflagration was a good forty miles away, and the ponderosa forest petered out at perhaps half of that distance. No, there would be no danger here. But this would be a grandstand seat for watching the smoke. It was turning gray and brown, which meant the fire was growing, spreading faster and farther than before. The plume towered aloft, and reached toward the camp, closer and closer. Then night fell.

With night came cooler temperatures and weaker wind. Both slowed the spread of the fire, and possibly gave the firefighters a chance to pinch it off, to build borders, firelines to contain and channel the fire, to reduce the forward edge to a narrower, and thus less destructive and easier to fight, front. But not to put it out, or even truly control it. The forest was too dry, and had not burned in far too long. It was thick, much too thick, with mature trees, and the ground below held deep duff, tinder-dry and resin-saturated pine needles, and far too many dead and dry branches and brush. Normally, an occasional fire every five or ten years would clear out the fire-burden, as it is called, without doing much actual damage. Now, it is a recipe for total incineration, leaving not a living tree standing. When this fire passes, it will leave a gray landscape of ashes and charcoal, dotted with snags, dead sentinels of the forest that was. It is not aspen country, it is too dry, but juniper can thrive here. In a decade or two, the late pine woods will be a forest of junipers. In their shade, the pines will sprout and grow, and eventually overshadow the junipers. It may take a century or two, but the pines will return. Eventually, only one who knows the signs will be able to tell this fire had been.

But now there is still trash to burn. Through the dawn's early light, the smoke that had faded in the twilight's last gleaming was still to be seen, a cloud, dirty white, on the southern horizon. It persisted through the morning, changing little, till the wind again resumed, stronger, if anything, than the day before. Again the smoke turned brown, and thickened, and loomed from the Southwest, bearing down straight for the campground. The smell was umissable. Throats and sinuses grew dry and irritated. And the fire was still almost forty miles away. Again the night cooled it, and the nocturnal winds died and ceased to fan the flames. But with the next dawn, hotter weather and higher winds carried the inferno to even greater intensity. Closer now, still more than thirty miles away, but after the twilight, a faint rosy glow could be discerned. The monster was very much alive.

The next dawn was more hopeful. The weather became cooler, the winds decreased greatly, and backed ninety degrees to the Southeast. That could be very good; if a strong fireline has been built on the western side, the fire might be controlled, at last. If the winds become too strong, and the fire jumps the line, it is only a couple of miles to a wide highway, the one I used in coming here. The wind would have to be very strong, and from an unusual direction, to jump *that* line! It could happen, but it offers a very good chance of containment. And even more auspicious, should the wind continue for a day or two, allowing the Eastern edge to be firmly established, then return to its prevailing southerly to westerly, the fire will be blown into acreage that is already burned over, and it will be controlled, contained, and soon extinguished. Hope is present.

But only hope, for the wind veered back to the Southwest, and blew even stronger than before. It is always something to consider here. Not thirty miles away, a wind gusting to one hundred eighty four miles per hour was once recorded. But wind always shifts for a reason; it is never random. This shift resulted from a change in the weather. It is much cooler, and the sky is unbroken overcast. There may be rain. Probably not much, not enough to extinguish the fire, but any rain will help. One can hope.

There was rain, a little, and it helped, but not much. What truly helped was weaker wind and cooler temperatures. Today the skies were clear, just a few clouds, but it got cold last night, and stayed cool all day. Some clouds were brownish, lightly tinged, and there was a bit of haze, but you needed a few miles of it to see that it was there. No smoke rose from behind the ridge. Not till evening. Then the plume could be seen. It was much smaller, and lighter, just a little gray, and that may be because the sun has set. The fire is a few miles farther east, but it is still there. A wildfire is a hard thing to kill.

The next day (yes, it just goes on and on), there was a slight haze on the far horizon, the forlorn tendrils of an exhausted fire. That is normal for a wildfire after a calm and cool night. I can see the fire teams (mind's eye, of course) frantically scrambling to get firebreaks built and threatening snags felled. By midafternoon there is a single towering column of smoke, white with age, rising straight up for several thousand feet before the top is carried off to the West. There is no wind at the base. When the winds do return, their only effect is to tilt the tower. The shifting and the cooling have been enough to doom this fire. Though the burn continues, hot and destructive, it is now all internal. The edges are contained, mile-wide firelines, built by the wildfire itself, prevent any further spread. The fire-teams ignore the blaze, letting it burn as it will (which it will do regardless of any action mere humans can take), concentrating on cooling the fire-lines, stamping out and drowning any remaining embers. In time, the last coals will grow dim, the last wisps of smoke will fade away. In time, the monsoon rains will turn the ash to mud and soak the minerals into the ground. New gullies will be carved until the roots of the sprouting grass and weeds again bind the soil. Then the trees will return.

We have learned from our mistake. Will our grandchildren remember the lesson? Will they let the replenished forest burn when it needs to? Or will they "protect" it as we did, till the entire forest vanishes in a week-long holocaust?

The road to Hell is paved with good intentions.

Morning Fire

Everyone knows and loves the campfire. The merry blaze that warms the hands and brightens the night, emphasizing the dark as it is driven back, providing peace and the sweet smell of wood-smoke, a chance to recapitulate the pleasures of the day, and to enhance adventures of other times, to tell tales taller than life, to speak of dreams and expand upon plans. The flames provide a cradle for imagination to kindle and grow, expanding with the rising smoke, maturing as the fire fades to embers, allowing the stars to shine through and lift the thoughts to the beckoning frontier. Campfires breed memories of toasted marshmallows and roasted knuckles, and reminiscences of the treasured times at CampWhatchamacallit, and poignant memorium of Old Bill who posed with a bison in Yellowstone, may he rest in peace. Campfires mean peace and security, in racial memories harking back twenty, forty thousand years, when fire was the sentry who warded off the wild wolves. The campfire symbolizes and epitomizes Camping; to most, it is the high point, for what could be better than the Evening Fire?

But there is something better. The hunters know of it, and many fishermen. It is the Morning Fire, the beginning of the New Day. My day begins at first light, even before the Shepherds' Dawn, when you can first distinguish a white hair from a black one. My fire was laid the night before, so all that is required is the flick of a lighter, and the tiny flame is born. The tinder warms the kindling and starts a billow of unseen smoke. The flames grow, and radiant heat begins to challenge the chill. A rapid rush of crackling and popping light surges

through the dry twigs and ignites the branches above, then bursts forth a welcome warmth bearing a cloud of fire flies, more ephemeral than mayflies, for they expire in only a second or two. The light reveals the smoke even as it ceases to form, and the bright flames arise, forcing the lightening sky to darken again, and driving me back as the initial fury consumes the fuel, rendering it to hot coals and ash as fluffy as snow. The leaping and bucking inferno fades to a proper, approachable size, a tame fire, broken to service. At this point the hungry hunter places a pot to boil his coffee, impatiently awaiting his first cup. I have never cared for coffee, so I am spared the torment of the modern man deprived of his automatic brewer and forced to endure the agonizing delay. On the other hand, I can never experience the ecstacy of the first sip. Such is life.

The air is cold, and frost glazes the darker surfaces. As I feed the fire, I relish the contrast. Many people enjoy the winter, the bite of the frigid wind, the sting on the cheeks, but a very large part of the pleasure derives from the knowledge that one can escape it at will. The howling blizzard is a satisfying thing when one is seated comfortably before a roaring fire in one's snug living room. One can smugly thumb the nose that the storm strives to frostbite. The same safety, lesser as the cold is lesser, but no less enjoyable, surrounds me here. The air is chill, but I am warm, for the fire that I created holds back the cold and weaves a nest of comfort around me. The comfort is in the warmth, but the satisfaction lies entirely in the mind.

Soon there are sufficient coals for cooking. I rise and mix the batter for a batch of bannock bread. The chill feels more intense after the contrast of the fire, and the warmth is all the better on my return. As the bread begins to bake, I gather eggs and bacon in the gathering light, and start my simple breakfast cooking. The smell of sizzling bacon teases me as the aroma of half-brewed coffee teases the hunter. A handful of green spruce needles salvaged from a recent slash pile are tossed in the fire to scent the smoke, and I break my fast on eggs and bacon, bannock and spring water. I think as I eat of the things I might do today, not planning my actions, just laying out options, savoring the possibilities, for I do not know which whims will take me at the opportune times. The sun gilds the western ridge, and the chill treasures its last fleeting moments as the first rays bring an instant warmth, dispelling the cold and thus the physical value of the fire; the spiritual worth remains, and my thoughts still mix with the dwindling flames. The fire subsides to mere embers, crumbling to white ash. Birds begin their morning songs. The first of the other campers begin to emerge. Their day is just beginning. Mine is well begun.

Light

Light has two qualities inherent in itself: Brightness and Hue. The variations and combinations of these are each infinite, and their interactions are infinite as well. And while these fairly well sum up the characteristics of light we see in an office or an apartment, they, infinite though they be, are far less than a half, or even a tenth, of the potentialities of light in the real world. For there is also a softness or a starkness and an ambience, a blending, a malleability, a contrast or concordance, when light shares the presence of life or rocks or water or air. The true quality of light is very much dependent on the environment in which it shines.

As the simplest example, the pure white light of an LED flashlight on a dark night shows the ground before you, all of the plants and pebbles as clearly as by day, but the illuminated area is *white*. There is an aura of whiteness that does not exist in sunlight. Yes, sunlight has more yellow, and thus it imparts a yellowish tinge or presence, and pure white will show the "true" colors. However, I am not talking about physics, but of the world. Physics is very limited; the World is infinite. What are the *true* colors of a meadow? The complete spectra as seen in the pure white light? The yellowish tint under the noonday sun? The reddish cast in the presence of a glorious sunset? Or the purple-gray pall in the gloom of heavy stormclouds?

Which is real? Which are the true colors?

All of them. Even the harsh independent hues in the artificed white light produced only by Man. That is thorough and complete, but no more real than the thorough and complete panoply of grays visible by the pale light of the full moon. The colors revealed under various lights are all true colors, because they are there, visible, you can see them. They are. The fact that things are is far more important, and true, than any reasons for their being, or reasons for their selves.

The dawn light, before the sun rises, is bright enough to reveal colors, bright enough, barely, to discern details, yet has a softness, not a haziness, not a lack of focus, though feeling like both. It is the effect photographers attempt to emulate with what they term "soft focus". Not quite in focus, not quite out. The dawn light lends an impression of hesitancy, as if the world has not yet decided to be there, a physical muzziness, a half-awake state in which the hidden dreams of the night still leave their last lingering touch, a residue of a different reality, as different as night from day. No instrument can measure it, for it is not there. It is not physical, it is mental, spiritual. It is not *there*; it is *here*.

When the sun rises from behind a ridge, the change is instantaneous. Where the rays strike directly, all is sharp and clear and bright. Trees are limned against the light, colored above and below, but deeply black against the sun. Stalks of grass that were a mass of palest brown are now individuals easily discerned. Bursting seed pods on slender stalks glow as if by self-emanated light. And the eastern slopes and the meadows, still shadowed, still enfolded in softness and clarity shrink and yield gradually to the golden glow. For the light is golden, and gold. It gilds the world in grandeur. The birds, who uttered only tentative chirps so shortly before, now pour out heartfelt songs, channeling the flood of gratitude flowing from the sun. Flowers unfold their petals that can now dazzle in the light, and every leaf slowly, ever so slowly, turns and twists and trims its surface to greedily, hungrily, absorb as much of the golden largesse as it can. The sun blesses the morning, and all rise, plants and animals and even the waters hazing into the air, accepting the benefice of fresh and new light, and energy, and life.

The sun is well up, half way to its zenith. It has clambered slowly up the steep slope of the sky, and now traverses the great plateau, nearly level, free of obstructions, for there is nary a cloud to be seen. The energy expended in the arduous ascent is now available for other tasks, and is strewn generously upon the world in brilliant beams, bouncing off rocks, skittering through aspen, scintillating on riffles and placidly floating on sleepy pools. Leaves and grasses gratefully drink it in, only the green sloppily splashing and dripping to the ground. The light is pure, pristine, taking as its own the clarity of the air. There is a feeling of life in the light, absent in the arid desert where the light of broad day is a tyrant, a fierce and omnipotent overlord from whom all things hide and cower in the shadows, but present in the forest where plants raise their limbs and wave happy hosannahs to their gracious and generous god, where insects sing in praise of the warmth, and only the deep shadows and the blood-thirsty predators of the night hide from his radiant face. And the mid-morning light *is* radiant, in every sense of the term. The light is happy, joyful, exuberant, and every thing it touches feels at least a touch of the same. There are characteristics of the light, when it bathes the forest or it sears the desert. We perceive them, we sense them. They are there. They are.

Noon. Not of the clock, but true noon, high noon, when the sun is as high as it will be, and shadows point due south. What there is left of them, for they are short, and small. Noon. The light is not the light of morning. It has lost the boisterous behavior of youth, and steadied in a settled pace. The day is mature, middle-aged, halfway through its threescore and ten quarter hours. The difference between the noon and the dawn is like to the difference between the father and his newborn seventh son. To the father, all is familiar; to the son, all is new. And their light reflects this. The plants lounge in a tranquil, almost bored relaxation. They have done a good morning's work, and now they feed on the unobstructed sunlight. The light is not too intense, not too hot (except in the desert, where it may kill a man or beast so impertinent as to stand unshielded in its unimpeded glare). It is there, but it does not obtrude upon us. Look in any direction you please, any direction except straight up. (And when was the last time you ever looked straight up?) The light is there, but it does not blind you, it does not impede vision in the slightest bit. It is simply there. A mother watches her child frolicking in the water, alert for the slightest sign of danger, but the happy child is oblivious, immersed in the game and the glory of splashing. Just as we, and the beasts and the birds, are immersed in the light, in the strongest, thickest, most *present* light of the day, but also immersed in the doings of the day, quite unaware of either immersion. Our attention is elsewhere, for the light does nothing to draw attention to itself. It is there, and that is its only characteristic. It is simply there.

The afternoon draws on. The sun is not hotter than it was at noon; in fact, it is growing less intense. But the work of warming the night-chilled Earth is done, and the heat that went into warming is now superfluous. But the surplus light still shines, and warms the air beyond bare need. The job is no longer interesting, it is old, it is mundane, it is tedious and boring. And the land reflects the attitude of the light. It is time to sleep, to siesta, to nap on the grass in the shade of a broad-spread oak, to let the body lie undisturbed while the spirit visits different realms near to hand, magical realms that run under rules of their own, realms where "fantasy" means this world where light assumes the attributes of matter and life and mind. Did you know this is a fantasy land? It is. It is a dream created by spirits, a playground where the most intricate and amusing games can be played, with the most nonsensical and hilarious rules imaginable. Rules that require that people do not fly, and water only runs downhill. Preposterous, but fun. Imagine, that light is more than simply vibrations of energy! But it is. It is far more, and right now, it is sleepy. Lethargic light, loafing through a languid afternoon.

In time, or in imagination (assuming they are different things), the day wanes. The sun trips over the edge of the plateau and plummits to the horizon. The fall towards dusk seems so much swifter than the rise from dawn. Perhaps it is because the morning hours stood alone, without earlier hours with which to compare them, and the evening hours are only a small fraction of the long and busy day. An hour in a day is much like a day in a life. To the child, a day lasts forever; to the man, it passes and is lost in the drawing of a breath. The evening light is in a hurry, having lazed through the afternoon, and now having to rush to get everything done. The sun is going on vacation, and the last-minute packing requires a frantic scrambling. The sun swells as it sucks up the light, reddening with the effort of gathering his child-beams, dancing and playing across the land. Then the rays realize the growing shadows have crept from their crypts and are skulking among the trees. The forests have grown dark, and darkness looms beneath the western ridges, threatening to block their retreat. A last desperate dash brings them to their father, to his warm embrace and safe shelter, and tranquillity is restored. As the sun touches the horizon, the land grows quiet and peaceful, as quiet as the light. The last lights lie soft on the land, as soft as the morning, yet different, more solid, more weighty, for this light leaves traces, remnants of all that has been and was done during the day.

And thus the light changes along with its environment. Some will say it is not the light that changes, that the light is immutable, and only the environment changes. But the two are inseparable, are part of each other. Just like matter and space, neither can exist without the other. The characteristics of light are what we perceive them to be, for no one can prove that the light even exists if we do not perceive it. Of course, that would mean that we could change the light simply by choosing to perceive it differently.

I'll tell you a secret: We can.

Light Show

Each year bears a common theme. This is the Year of Weather.
A couple of months ago I experienced the most torrential
downpour I have ever seen. Yesterday I saw the biggest
hailstones of my life (and unbeknownst as yet to me, they will
be dwarfed by the hailstones tomorrow). Today it is lightning.
I heard it once, in another year, in another state, thunder that
rumbled without pause for more than sixteen minutes. Today I
have seen it.

Lightning! Flashes near and far! Ground strikes and
cloud-to-cloud. Bolts five miles distant and five hundred feet
away, and every foot between. Frequent flashes, not more than
three seconds apart, usually only one, on and on, for half an
hour and more, and more, without break. God is holding a
press conference in the clouds, and the recording angels are
taking flash photos. The thunder is continuous, often so loud it
drowns the drumming of the raindrops. It is night, so the flares
of light destroy night vision, and the effect is of a celestial
strobe light, the devil's disco, stark black and vivid white that
vanishes in an instant to an ebony as solid as wood, over and
over, falling rain standing motionless in mid-air, trees not
swaying, but in different positions every second, clouds a
turgid irregular mass of static swirl. This is chaos. This is an
unpredictable and irrational denial of logic and experience.
This is nothing that ever was or ever could be. Sure, the mind
understands what is happening and why, but the senses do not.
There is a distinct lag, a pause, between seeing and hearing,
feeling and comprehension, the sorting out of reality. It is like

the eye of a hurricane at sea. That is the only place I have seen lightning at all like this, but it was all in the wall of the eye, not everywhere, as I see it now. But the surface of the sea in the eye! It is not, as Hollywood portrays, a dead calm. Yes, the air is still, but the sea is a chaos of waves, storm swells coming from literally every direction, meeting, cancelling, reinforcing. Often they do not manifest as rolling waves, but as sudden mountains rising fifty, eighty, a hundred feet straight up, or as instant pits, tiger traps opening with absolutely no warning, abysses eighty feet deep. It is not at all possible to predict or anticipate how the water will move, will change, from one moment to the next. Thus it is now with the rain and the wind and the lightning and the clouds. They are what they are and they do what they do and it is beyond imagination what they will do next, because they change too rapidly, they are always two steps ahead of perception. And then it slows. Like a motor whose battery is slowly running out of charge, the pace declines. The flashes become less frequent, the rumbles more random, the rain less resonant, the wind less wild. Slower. Slower. Raindrops become discrete, separate strikes easily counted. The wind wanes to nothing. Lightning becomes rare, and only in the East.

The storm endured for an hour, but now it is ending. A few final flickers, a tap or two to say "Farewell". The stars appear, and order is restored, as if it was never broken.

Water

Water

We have all seen streams and brooks and rivers, ponds and lakes and, many of us, oceans. We have even looked at them, noticed them. I have written of them many times, from many viewpoints. But never about the one thing common to them all, the water itself.

Water is unique. It is endlessly protean. It can be gaseous, vapor, like Air, *part of* the air. It can be solid like Earth, frozen, in one great slab or in infinite tiny crystals. It can even, when heated to a plasma state, be indistinguishable from Fire. And it can, as itself, be liquid. It can take on any shape, any size. It can lie as still pools, or move, slowly or swiftly, as streams and rivers. It can lie still and at the same time be in motion, as the great swells in the sea. And it can fly, or float, as clouds and fog, which do not consist of water vapor, but of actual liquid water, water so finely divided as to comprise clouds (literally) of the tiniest droplets, only distinguishable from raindrops in their size.

Let us look at a part, a small part, of what water can do. It can quietly lie in still pools, moving only on the surface, and even then, just barely, possibly ruffled by a breeze to form ripples on the surface, yet often utterly still, forming a perfect mirror.

It can flow, a large mass, slowly, silently, smoothly and serenely, calmly winding its way through valleys and across plains, a home for fish and frogs, a larder for birds and raccoons, slaking the thirsts of flora and fauna for many miles.

Or it can flow energetically, vaulting limberly over submerged obstructions in a series of standing waves, the body of water speeding past while the wave itself remains utterly stationary.

Water can partially climb up an obstruction, then slip off to the side, leaving the boulder or log permanently blanketed in a thin silent wave, an inverted dimple with neither turbulence nor tiny bubbles to attract attention.

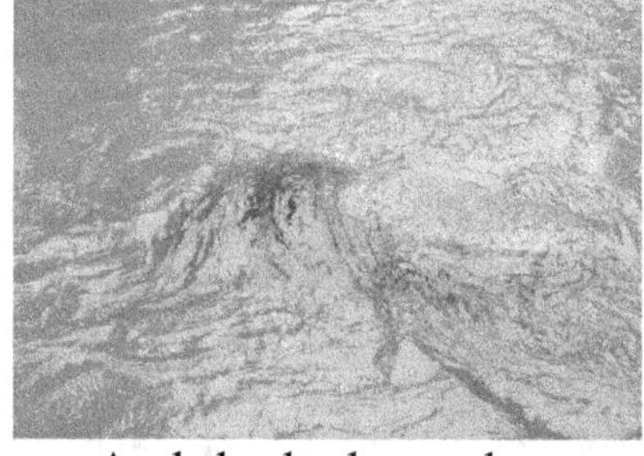

And the bed may be very steep, forcing the water to fall in a series of small steps, or in one continuous cascade, forty, fifty, sixty degrees of slope, not enough to merit the label "fall", but too much to allow the name of "rapids". White water, even when it is only inches deep, unnavigable by even the most skilled rafter. Or the flow can be vertical, hundreds, thousands of feet.

Always it is beautiful. Transparent, green, deep blue, night black, mud brown, frothy white, or silvery mirror. Even the raging torrent that has washed away the bridge and bars your path is savagely beautiful. Perhaps a heavily polluted stream bearing floating garbage and a loud stench will be foul and offensive, but it is not the water that is at fault. Water is not mild or angry, merciful or vicious. Playful, perhaps. It is an elemental power, knowing and caring nothing for us or for our likes and dislikes, our goals and dreams. If it has any desires, it only wishes to flow, swiftly and unimpeded, but it will take every barrier as an opportunity, and, if it is at all possible, will use the barrier as a toy. Watch the water as it leaps and bounds from rock to rock, listen to it fizzing in the frothy pool at the base of a fall. It is laughing. Listen to the brooks singing a playful tune. Listen to the happy raindrops improvising a beatnik tone poem on needles and leaves and puddles and ponds.

And yet, it is only water. It is one of the simplest and commonest chemicals in the world. We cannot exist without it; all life as we know it is absolutely dependent on water. But even if Life did not need it, even if it was not crucial to shaping the lands and controlling the climates, what a dull and dreary world it would be if there were no water. Such a world would be like a child without laughter, like a sky without stars, like a universe without color. Like the surface of the Moon.

Truly, water is a wonder-full thing.

Falling Water

What is it about falls that fascinates us so? Why do they excite our admiration, do they capture our attention and captivate our imagination? It is only water, falling. Niagara Falls, the only outlet of four of the Great Lakes, channelled through one solitary sluice, massive, roaring, pounding, on and on and never stopping. Okay, that is impressive, simply because of scale, it is so huge. And while it actually did stop, once, in a winter so cold that the Falls froze solid, that was even more impressive, because it was so rare, so unexpected, almost unbelievable. But Bridal Veil Falls in Utah, why is that so great? The water falls a long way, much farther than Niagara, but it is not that much water. From a short distance, you can hardly tell the water is moving, it is only some white streaks on a cliff. If you diverted the water and painted the channels white, no one would give it a second glance. But as it is, it is beautiful!

Falling waters. We love it. We make it wherever we can. The Romans channeled water for hundreds of miles to supply their cities, but when the water arrived, did they use it? No, first they threw it up in the air just so they could watch it come down. *Then* they drank it. People have been doing this for thousands of years, building fountains so they could watch and listen to the falling water. It is a sure sign of intelligence, of sapience: Throwing water in the air, just to see it come down.

Yes, we listen to it. We cherish the sound. Think of all of the poems and songs and odes to falling rain, to rushing waters, to brooks that babble and burble and murmur and plash. We listen to the water, and we all hear the voices, we all hear the words that we do not understand, that leave us no wiser, but still we listen. Perhaps it harks back to our infancy, when Mother held us to her breast, and crooned to us and talked to us. We heard the words, but did not understand them. No, that is not quite true. The words carried meaning; they meant warmth, and peace, and love, and all is right with the world. We could slumber in safety, and all would be well. The water-sound is like that; it means peace and tranquillity.

And what of the water, the falling, the flow? Even in silence, the beauty remains.   It falls, it flies, it leaps and bounds, dancing, frolicing, crashing on crags and shattering to scores of scintillating sparkles, unharmed, undiminished, immortal, invulnerable, laughing over tragedies that merely tickle, constantly changing while staying exactly the same, from the lip of the falls to the pool at their base, shrieking with utter delight, then flowing placidly away, chuckling quietly as if to say "Ah, that was refreshing!" And refreshing it is.

The scummy stagnant pool stinks, its flavor is vile, it can sicken and kill you with a single sip. But let the water flow down a fall, let it leap over stones and dance in the riffles, slip through the sands, and magically, it is pure and sweet.

The fall of water is magic, pure magic. It cleans the body while it purifies the soul. It soothes the ear and fascinates the eye. It is immortal and it is immutable. It is Life. Perhaps it is not alive. Perhaps it has no soul of its own. Perhaps. I do not know. And it does not matter. Water is life, water is spirit. Water reigns supreme, for life cannot be without it, and even the strongest stone crumbles before it. Water is eternal, it is patience, and it is strength. We see ourselves in the falling water. We see all things, for they are all there.

In the water, we see our selves.

Hail

There was hail two days ago. Not *too* bad, nickel size and smaller. It tore one small rip in my tent fly, easily repaired with duck tape. I care little, for the tent is eight months old, worn and weakened by the strong sunlight of deserts and of high altitude, and due for replacement. The hail also provided ice for my cooler. And it was wonderful to watch. But today, . . .

It had been sunny all morning, warm, not even breezy. It started clouding up a bit around noon, and now, three hours later, a few drops of rain scent the fields. Anything that could be water-damaged is already in the tent, and the firewood is covered by a tarp. I move my chair in, and relax to enjoy the show. I do not expect a thriller. A pleasant short subject, *The Adventures of Pitter Patter*, only lasts a few minutes. Then a flash of lightning and a roll of thunder announce the main feature: *Hailstorm II: Just When You Thought It Was Safe.*

The usual vanguard of eighth-inch and quarter-inch pebbles leapt and danced on ground and grass and rattled a riff on the roof. The nickel and dime crew came next, laughing and littering the landscape. The fly can only take so much. Should I shift the tarp, guard my gear at the cost of dampened firewood? I had just decided to make the sacrifice when the storm troopers arrived, the big guns, the barrage of the heavy artillery. A hole appeared, and another, and a third. With my thick bike jacket over my head, I scrambled into the storm and swept the tarp off the wood and over the tent, no longer to protect the tattered fly, but to ward the rain from off my now unprotected possessions. Not two minutes elapsed before I was back under cover, zipping the door shut and mopping up the spillage with my dirty laundry. I was in time; the worst bit of damage was a dampened notebook; my sleeping bags were dry. Then I looked up.

The fly is finished; a dozen holes and rips, some seam-to-seam. The porch overhang is shredded, gone. The tarp keeps the rain out, but the hailstones *rumble* on the roof. How big are they? I notice a couple of bruises on my hands. I look outside, but between the rain and mist and motion, I cannot discern the size of the stones. But they are big. Well, I have patience. When the storm is over, we shall see. For now, I am warm and dry, and the spectacle is - - - well, spectacular. Impressive.

And now it is done. All precipitation has ended, the clouds are breaking up, the sun shines from the West. And the

fog rises. I have not seen fog in at least a year, unless you count being in a cloud. But that is not the same as true fog; true fog is more than just another cloud at ground level. Clouds fly in the air, and belong to the Sky; fogs lie on the ground, and belong to the Earth. The ground is almost completely covered with ice as far as I can see, and it chills the air, condensing the moisture. Hailfog, thick fog, feeding on the heavy humidity from the rain. The streaming sunlight does not burn off this fog; it will persist as long as the ice remains, for the ice chills the air as fast as the sun warms it. And it will remain for some time. Over half of the stones are larger than a quarter, many are well over an inch. There have been larger hailstones, much larger, but these are the 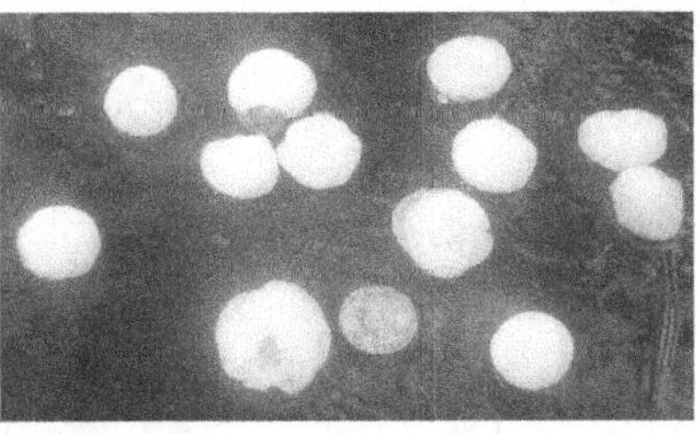 biggest I have ever seen outside of pictures. And they lie in drifts, some over a foot deep. A pair of pickup trucks have parked under trees to sit out the storm. One starts to leave, but cannot, the wheels will not grip. It is like trying to drive on marbles. The driver curses, laughs, shakes his head, and kills the motor. My bike is unharmed, because I parked it where it would be safely shielded by the wide branches of a Ponderosa Pine. None of my gear, aside from the fly, is damaged at all. The grass still stands. The trees are fine. I have read of hailstorms stripping branches bare of leaves, but pine, fir and spruce appear to be almost immune. Even the aspen, with their twisting, dancing, limber leaves, have suffered no harm.

But not Man. I stroll through the campground. Here is a car, fully exposed, facing the West from whence the storm came. The windshield is starred, the hood bears dozens of dents. There is a tent, reduced to rags dangling from hoop poles, several inches of ice soaking the sleeping bags within; the owners will be appalled when they return, the more so because, wherever they may be, they probably did not even experience rain, for these mountain thunderstorms are very local phenomena. Here is a picnic table half covered with broken glass jars. There a man kneels atop his motor home, tossing off plastic pieces of a shattered skylight. Here is a party that I saw arrive at noon, packing up and leaving, their weekend wasted. I tell them there will likely be no more such storms, that the weather pattern is changing. But they do not believe me. Their son does, but that kind of people never listen to children. And here are two couples, laughing and joking. They came on bicycles, arrived and finished pitching their tents just as the first drops fell. If they had arrived just ten minutes later... As it is, they are among the very few, perhaps the only ones, who have suffered no damage at all.

The ice is melting, a myriad streams trickling through the grass, making a morass of mud and a river of the road. The sun is bright, so the air above is warm, and that which is chilled by the spheres of ice flows away downhill. I want a fire to drive off the chill and damp, so I whittle for a few minutes, then tuck the dry shavings under damp twigs and surface-sodden logs. The ignorant laugh; wiser ones watch with interest. Two feet of wadded duck tape under it all lights quickly and burns long, and in ten minutes the flames are dancing merrily. Some go and apply the lesson, and in half an hour, happy campfires blaze all around. The sadder sites stink of burned fire-lighter, but show no surviving flames.

Ignorance always exacts a price.

Horror

Stephen King writes horror, and he is quite good at it. He knows to not write too much detail, that the greater part of the horror lies in the mind and imagination of the reader. But he does not write the most intense, the most horrifying horror. He writes fiction. I have seen horror, a deluge of horror so intense that, while I can write of it and describe it, even in minute and accurate detail, still the greater part will come from you, from your mind and imagination. And even then, it will not equal what I saw.

It was in the deep desert, a land so dry the brush, when there was brush, never spaced themselves less than ten feet apart. Usually there was only an occasional cactus, sometimes a rarer skeletal bush. The land was flat, dead flat, all the way to the mountains twenty or thirty miles off. All sand and sun, broiling hot at noon, freezing cold at dawn. Literally freezing, but there was no frost. There was no moisture to freeze.

The desert is a place of illusion; nothing is truly what it seems. The land is barren and lifeless, and nothing moves, but the nothing leaves tracks for the observant to see. Non-existent lakes shimmer a mile or so away. Always a mile or so away. Walk towards them all day long, and they are still just a mile or so away. Clouds darken the horizon, but never move, for they are not clouds. They are mountains, or the tops of mountains, a horizon farther away than the horizon itself. Sand lies smooth, flat, unbroken, except that it is cut by deep gullies that are utterly invisible from a hundred feet away. Gullies that bear all the sign of having been carved by streams, by rivers, here where there are no streams, not even intermittent or subterranean, for such are marked by lines of brush, or at least cottonwoods, and these gullies are as bare of life as the peaks of the alps.

I was looking into one of these gullies. It was time to make camp, for the moon was setting, and soon the sun would rise and scorch the land. I wanted shade, any shade, even a blanket suspended from my staff. There was a soft, sandy floor aorund the rocks in the gully, and a steep embankment on the southwest side, a place of cool shade in the hottest part of the day. Relatively cool. But here, even slightly cool is something to be sought. It looked like a good campsite. There was even a fire-ring containing fragments of charcoal, where others had recently found this place and used it, sheltered from wind, shaded from sun. Others who knew little of the desert. Lucky ones, in that they had escaped the trap, had survived. Or more accurately, they had survived for a while; they may never have reached their intended destination. But do not look for the campsite, for it is no longer there.

The trap beckoned, and lied to me, "Come! Come rest, out of the sun, out of the wind, in peace, and quiet, and comfort, and safety." The siren song was tempting, for the odds were very heavily in my favor, and the site appeared so perfect, so complete, almost flawless. Almost. But that one flaw...

The stakes were too high. I made camp a dozen yards away, pinning my blanket to a lonely saguaro, and weighting the base with rocks from the gully. I gathered broken bits of wood, also from the gully. Driftwood, half-buried in sand. It was enough for a fire, enough to cook dinner, and breakfast in the evening. I slept in the shade. Twice the heat wakened me, and I moved my blanket a bit to make a new shade. In the late afternoon, I awoke, uneasy. The heat was great, the sunlight bright, the air as still as I have ever known. I seemed to hear something, very low, almost a thunder, a rumble, but when I sat up, there was nothing. All was still, as still as... death?

I listened. I heard nothing. Nothing at all. I could see no movement, just sand and rocks, and a very few plants. Clouds. Overhead, all around, the sky was purest blue, untainted, but there were clouds among the mountains, far, far off. It could be raining there, for all the difference it might make to me. As I watched, I could almost hear the thunder. Steady thunder, more like a freight train in the far distance. A sound like one's imagination creates to fill the unacceptable silence. Probably the blood rushing in my ears, the so-called sound of the sea one hears in a conch shell. But it grew louder, and I knew it was not imagination.

I stood near the rim, on the inside of a bend, looking down on the siren campsite. Without my volition, imagination placed me in the gully, sleeping beside the smoking embers in the old fire-ring, my head pointing upstream with the slightly higher elevation, comfortable in the shadow of the bluff bank, twelve feet below the desert surface. In the world of real, I watched the Wall approach, a pile of mud eight, maybe nine feet high, rolling rocks and tumbling trunks amid mud-smeared branches and splashing brown, pouring at thirty or forty miles per hour, wrenching at the walls and eradicating the campsite, filling the gully to within a few feet of the rim with thin mud or deeply-colored water, roiling, leaping, splashing, scaring me back in fear of the land being snatched from beneath my feet. The roar swept on, the banks changed shape. The mud deepened then became more shallow as it faded into water, still brown, but less so, and now undoubtedly water. It flowed on, I do not know how long - five minutes, ten, an hour. It imprisoned my attention, and I never even thought of moving. I have seen

Niagara Falls, I have seen the eye of a hurricane. Stronger they are, far more powerful, but they lacked this suddenness, this savagery. Nature does not care, has no sympathy or empathy for our harsh pains and sufferings, and certainly no hostility, no evilness. She feels no joy or satisfaction about the injuries she inflicts upon our meager bodies. So I have seen, and so I have long believed. But now... If there was any Nature in Stalin or Hitler, in Torquemada or Bernard Gui, it was this, it was the flash flood.

Had I slept in that camp, I would not have woken, save possibly to a second or two of cold, sodden, dark brown terror, hopefully with no understanding at all of the dread devastation overwhelming me. Or worse, had I woke and scrambled to get out, I would have been swept aside, to be flung to the surface and bandied about until the rolling rocks tore and ground me apart, drowned and crushed and drawn and quartered, all at once in an eternal instant of pain and anguish. And none would have known of my terrible fate. The fragments of my limbs would have been buried in the mud or devoured by grateful scavengers, with not a trace left to hint at the tale. It would only be known that I had walked into the desert, and had not emerged. And none would have wondered. None would have been surprised.

The desert is like that.

The Secret of the Water Sound

I have found a fine spot to sit in the gentle sun at the very brink of a shaded creek. It is about fifteen feet wide here, shallow and rocky. Just thirty feet upstream it is only three feet wide, swiftly leaping down a series of foot-high falls. Twenty feet downstream it smoothly drops five feet in a twenty-foot stretch. It is very talkative.

Yes, the waters talk. But you have to listen, and carefully, deeply. There is a very good reason for "babbling brook" and "murmuring stream" to be such cliches: the brooks and streams *do* babble and murmur. They speak many languages. Each *stream* speaks many languages. Some are smooth and liquid, Spanish, where water runs through a bed of reeds. There is a gutteral Germanic where the flow over three-foot rocks has carved deep holes as it plunges. A swift stream over six-inch stones speaks a sort of tinkling fairy Chinese. The rushing escape between two blocking boulders is pure Scandinavian, while multitudinous paths through a logjam or debris dam are almost a muttered Swahili. Every person will hear different languages. Every ear is different, every perception unique. To a large degree, you will hear what you expect to hear, what you let yourself hear, even what you want to hear.

Off to my left I hear what could be a radio talk-show host, a mellow, persuasive voice. It continues, steadily, without a break or a pause for breath, in an unhurried run-on sentence, clearly precise, but I never can quite make out a single word. Now that I notice, off to my right is another voice, the guest, perhaps, a bit deeper, a bit slower, but just as persuasive, just as persistent. I feel I would have to agree with him, if I could only understand his words. And there, across the stream, a female guest, sort of a soprano, chattering, almost breathless. Then a trout breaks the surface, and shatters the spell. The talk show is gone, replaced by a broken drone, a non-repetitive glooping, and a random patter.

The creek begins chanting. Chill the room? Fill it soon? There is no sense to it, but there is, almost. It can never hold meaning until you put it there, or feel it there, or find it there, and then it means . . . No, I mustn't tell you; you have to find it for yourself.

Weather

Coolth

I stayed a week at Upper Tonto Creek campground, lying at 5600 feet. It was mid-June, a bit late for that place, and temperatures were unseasonably warm. The nights were pleasant, dropping to the mid-60s. I still used a sleeping bag, but unzipped to act as only a blanket. Even so, it was still too warm to use it at all till several hours after sunset. The mornings were pleasant, but not invigorating, for about five hours. Then around nine-thirty or ten it became necessary to seek shade. It was a good time to watch and to write, for a few hours. When the heat rose to the high nineties, it was time for an hour of nap, then down to the creek to one of several swimming holes. I know a couple that the fisherman do not use, because the only way to reach them is to hike a ways through the stream itself. They are wonderful places to lie down and let the cool water flow over, under, around you. I always bring my camera and notebook, for one never knows when a special beauty will arise or the Muse will visit. I return to camp refreshed about the time the sun is dipping behind the western ridge, warm again and already dry, even if the pool was only a quarter mile from camp. I visit a while with the neighbors or the Camp Host, if any are present, then prepare dinner. Sometimes we have a sort of pot luck, such as I cook a few batches of bannock, another cooks a dessert, and a third fries up a mess of fish he caught today. Then to bed around dark, or socialize for an hour or two by the fire, or maybe lie back and take a stroll among the stars. It is good. It is *very* good. But it has been good for a week, and the weather is getting hotter. It is not boring, but it is becoming jading. I am ready for a change.

So today I packed my gear and headed east, and up. Following the Mogollen Rim, I left the Tonto National Forest for the Sitgreave, passed through tiny towns, Heber, Overgaard, Clay Spring, Pinedale, getting steadily higher and cooler. Linden is bigger, Show Low is huge, it even has traffic lights! Then the towns diminish, Pinetop, Lakeside, McNary. I pass through the White Mountain Apache Reservation and enter the Apache National Forest. A dozen miles, then off the paved road and another mile to Winn campground.

Winn is beautiful! It is thickly inhabited by aspens with the successor pines starting to shade them out. It is far enough from the road that you never hear a motor, even when the wind is from the West. The nearest settlements are too far away for their small looms to be detectable. The campground borders on a meadow of many acres, over which the bugles of elk drift through the whispers of pines and the rustles of aspens. We stand above ninety-three hundred feet. A rise of thirty-seven hundred feet has dropped the highs to the mid seventies, and the lows to about fifty. It is a whole new world, with different trees, different smells, different sounds, and cool, delicious cool. And to top it off, I get site forty-seven, right next to the meadow. I *always* get site forty-seven. I think it is the best one, but apparantly no one else does. Strange. Well, they say there is no accounting for taste.

Clouds drift down from the North, to pack the South with solid gray. Thunder rumbles from the Southwest, though I have only seen one flash. The weather radio says fifty percent chance of thunderstorms for the next four days; the Monsoon is starting. Tomorrow, weather permitting, I will gather firewood from the slashpiles that amply dot the campground. Perhaps I should do it today, but the cool and quiet feels so good, and it looks like rain very soon. Besides, I can handle wet firewood. I will be content to sit through several long storms, for it has been months since I have seen a good rain, and the forests badly need it. For now, I am content to steep my body in the cool and quiet, to get re-acquainted with the squirrels and ravens and aspens and pines, old friends who remember me from days gone by. The rain begins, a few miniscule drops, tiny taps teasing and twitting, hinting of what may come, and may not. You can never be sure with mountain weather. But I do not know, and do not care. I enjoy the thunder. I love the rain. If the sky clears, I will watch the stars, for this is one of the best spots in Arizona for stargazing. I will quietly revel in whatever comes till the Fourth of July. By then, I should be beginning to feel jaded again, and ready for another change. Then I shall head north. I have a long journey ahead, and it is going to be very cool.

Contrary Clouds

I picked the wrong place to camp.

It's been raining the past two days. I knew it was coming and, while I can ride in the rain, having the skills and gear, I prefer to make camp and wait it out in comfort. I'm in no hurry to get anywhere. I picked what seemed a good site; a small knoll with good drainage, tall trees near enough to distract lightning, far enough away to not threaten. Plenty of wood, good view.

But now the rain has ended, the cold front has passed. The air is a bit chill, but the sun is out, warm and pleasant, when the clouds don't block it. And there lies the problem. I am in the mountains, and mountain clouds are peculiar. On the plains, you can watch a cloud rise on the western horizon, sail steadily across the sky, and descend into the east; it may change shape a bit, but it stays pretty much the same size and color all of the way. Not so in the mountains. Updrafts and downdrafts create a roiling chaos in the sky. Out of nothing, a tiny wisp of white forms in the clear blue. It drifts south, growing and changing shape. It expands to fifteen, twenty, thirty degrees across, with another wisp forming behind it. Still ambling steadily south, it dwindles and evaporates, vanishing before it can touch on the horizon. It is a continuous procession of small clouds treading the same path across the heavens, as if it was a fenced lane for celestial cattle.

And the sun sits right in the middle of the road. A mile or so to the southeast, across the lake, the land is bright and unshadowed. Here, I get a minute or two of sensuous warmth, then ten or fifteen minutes of cold shade. Still, one can truly appreciate those short surges of sunlight; the contrast with the cold makes them all the more pleasant. The warming land will alter the air currents. The sun will cross the lane and bathe my camp in a continuous glow. In a few hours, I may be seeking shade, or having a glorious nap in the middle of a meadow.

Perhaps this is the right place to camp. Very right, indeed.

Interlude in the Night

It was a dark and stormy night. At least, it threatened to be.
The weather was warm, the breezes were gentle. Conditions
were nearly perfect for sleeping under the stars. Except the
chances favored rain. I carry a little bivy tent for just such
times. I did not want to bother with my usual tent, since I was
probably only going to be here one night; it takes about twenty
minutes to pitch the tent, and fifteen to strike it, plus it has to
be carefully folded and loaded on top of the trailer. Call it forty
minutes in all. The bivy should, theoretically, require no more
than fifteen, maybe twenty, all told.

I had never used the bivy before. It is just a little thing,
eight feet long, about three wide and two and a half tall. There
is just room for a sleeping bag and a small space for stuff like
flashlight, glasses and chamber jug. Pitching it took nine
minutes fifty-six seconds. First time, except when I had just
bought it. (Only a complete tyro will buy a tent and not pitch it
till its first use. It can be quite amusing, and a bit pathetic, to
watch some tenderfeet learning to pitch their tent. In the dark.
Or rain. Or both.) With practice, I would get the pitching time
down to maybe six minutes. Except I will not have the chance.

Once the tent was pitched, I laid out a light foam pad, then
my sleeping bag. That was difficult and time consuming. I
found A) I can not crawl into the bivy on my hands and knees,
as my hips are too high and wide for the top of the door, B)
once inside, I can *not* turn around, and C) I cannot back in,
because my hips are too high and wide for the top of the door.
So, to get in, I have to sit down in front of the tent, stick my

legs in, and worm my way forward. Oh, yes: Take my shoes off first, as they are very hard to reach once I am inside. There is also no room to store any gear; that has to stay outside, out of the weather or under a tarp.

All things considered, the bivy saves little time, and that is more than offset by a lot of inconvenience. I once described a tent as "more a garment, a large coat with big pockets, than a structure or shelter"; to extend the analogy, the bivy is more a girdle than a tent. For backpacking, the bivy is a good thing, because it is very light. For any other mode of travel, a small dome tent would be better, and my canvas wall tent would be just as good. Live and learn.

I must admit, though, once the bivy was well pitched and furnished and I was inside, barefoot, it was quite comfortable. A bit too small, because in rolling over, I was almost sure to press on a wall, which would be covered in condensation from my breath, and if it was raining, would probably cause a leak. (Yes, fabric tents *do* leak if you touch them, unless they are fully waterproof. Or it is not raining.) I slept quite thoroughly till about midnight, when the fun began.

You see, there *was* a storm, and a big one. Not big in the sense of intense, but big in square miles. A lightning storm that stretched to all horizons, or, as Lewis Carroll would describe it, wabe. Wabe, meaning it goes a long way before, and a long way behind, and a long way beyond on each side. Lightning flashed from all directions, mostly cloud-to-cloud, and the thunder was a constant quiet rumble. Inside the tent I could see strobing flashes, more often light than dark, there were so many of them, and the sound was an almost uniform background. For many minutes, this was all. Then the first patter of the raindrops came, and slowly grew till it was a constant tattoo on the tent. I know not how long the rain fell, for the lullaby soon soothed me into slumber. Some two hours later I was awakened by a burglar, an inquisitive hungry racoon stealing a meal, or trying to. My cooking area smelled of food, and the little thief was turning over tools and pilfering among pots, but there was no prize for him tonight. Almost none, for I had inadvertently left my cookie jar out. It is a plastic coffee can, and I had overlooked it when I retired for the night. Little RJ knocked it to the ground and was rolling it, like a barrel, off into the night. Now, I do not mean he was randomly knocking the jar about, hoping it would move in the general direction he desired. No, he had it on its side, correctly aligned, and was pushing it, just as a man would push a keg. He knew exactly what he was doing. How he would open it once he reached his destination, I do not know, and I doubt he did, either, but we were both completely certain he would find a way. While I do not particularly mind him getting a few cookies, that jar was valuable and, not being a coffee drinker, it might be a long time before I obtained another jar as good as that one, so I squirmed out of the tent and arrested him. Well, I arrested his theft. Poor thing, he found no food at my camp, and in the end the only thing he managed to steal was off into the woods.

It was still night, and darker than before, for there was no more lightning, but not stormy, for all of the clouds were gone, washed from the sky, and the stars gleamed through the freshly laundered air. The ground was damp, and the aromas of forest, flower and grassland drifted through warm air. I had not had my full quota of sleep, but the silent world was just so perfect, and the first dawn so near, I simply sat back to enjoy it.

I can always take a nap or two later.

Distant Lightning

We are all familiar with distant thunder, the muted rumble of a lightning storm invisible on the far side of the horizon. It will intrude upon our attention. We do not have to be facing in the correct direction, we do not have to concentrate or pay it any attention. The sound pervades the area. It may be loud enough to command immediate recognition, or it may be so soft, we have to puzzle and classify before we know it for what it is.

Lightning is usually just as intrusive. The flashes are generally bright enough to startle, and usually are accompanied by their thunderous soundtracks. But not tonight. The sun had set, and the last twilight was just fading away. The sky was cloudless, except far off to the Northwest, where a long bank protruded five or ten degrees above the horizon. It was mostly obscured by trees, but there was one spot where there were no obstructions between us. I was strolling there, enjoying the cool and quiet, when the distant gray cloud, which I had not before noticed, turned pink. Solid pink, the whole thing, a bit mottled where the clouds were thicker, and it lasted less than a second. It was enough to arrest my attention, to freeze me in my tracks, to stare, expecting, hoping, for more. And there was more. The same phenomenon, a bit to the North, but orange instead of pink. Then yellow, a double flash. Again and again, at four or ten second intervals, pink and red and orange and yellow. I never saw a bolt of lightning, never could tell if it was cloud-to-cloud or ground-to-cloud. The flashes were all erratic, never predictable, they could come at any interval and at any location, and there was never a sound, never a hint of thunder. A few of the brightest yellows were enough to light the trees around me, slightly. It was much like watching a color organ synchronized to music, except the musicians were thoroughly incompetent. It was highly arresting, enchanting, mesmerizing. At least, it was for me. I pointed it out to a passing camper, commenting on the rare beauty of it. He glanced at it and said "Yeah". Then he walked off.

Lightning is very common. Bolts falling in the distance or nearby, clear and sharp or blurred by intervening rain. Perhaps the best is in hail, where the frosted white stones flash on all sides, tiny sparks, frigid reflections of the intense fury. Flares rising from the ground into the clouds are brightest and most clearly defined, dramatic discharges, each one of which could power a village all day, if we could only capture it. Lightning leaping between clouds is most illuminating, not so bright as a ground strike, but more diffused, more effective in demolishing the dark. Thunder is even more common, for it is rare to see lightning and not hear thunder, but common for thunder to roll over the horizon, to bounce from hillside to hillside, many miles from its invisible source. The silent cloud lightning is much more rare. At least, perceiving it is rare. It is far over the horizon, so the clouds must be at high altitude, pushing the limit where thunderheads can exist. Thus it appears low, and is usually obscured by intervening hills and trees. And being so far off, its thunderous crash, just as loud as the bolt that strikes next to you, has faded and been absorbed by many miles of intervening matter. It does little to attract attention to itself. And rarity, as we all know, enhances value, at least the perceived value of good things.

To see the distant lightning, you must be in the right place, at the right time, under the right conditions, and facing in the right direction. It is much like an intermittent sunset, a set of transient glows, as if the sun were being switched off and on. It is rarely seen as more than a slight glow. This one was intense, more than any I had seen before.

It is sights such as this that make life in the mountains so worthwhile.

Not In Kansas Anymore

Never trust mountain weather. It is as unreliable as a common politician. The pristine sky is clear, and the night is perfect for starwatching. Eventually you go to bed, only to awaken to the drumming of rain on the roof. But at dawn the sky is again clear. Or you depart your campsite for an afternoon of hiking, and return all sweaty from the constant hot sun to find your tent lies in tattered shreds and your sleeping bag is buried under six inches of hailstones. The weather can change in minutes, and will rain on one side of a hill while the other remains bone dry.

I expected rain tonight. It is almost always possible, but this time the weather service agreed. So I made camp early enough to get set up and gather a few days' worth of firewood, which I carefully stowed beneath a tarpaulin. I even laid a fire and left it covered, ready to light instantly in the morning. I often mention that I am lucky, but I find in most cases, luck is something you make yourself. This evening I was very lucky.

I had expected a cool morning, possibly as low as the mid-thirties, and damp, so my long underwear was laid out and ready. When I awoke, however, the temperature felt much lower, well below freezing, in fact. I hauled the long johns into the sleeping bag to pre-warm them, and slipped into them before emerging. Dressing quickly, I opened the tent. I saw Montana in July. The firs cloaked the hills on three sides of the dale, and walled off the mouth on the fourth side, but I could barely see them. The dirt road winding through, and the grassy meadow were no longer in sight. The brook was there, no longer silvery, but black, in sharp contrast to the gleaming white it now cut through. It had not rained last night, it had snowed. Several inches covered the ground and cloaked the trees and tent, and the snow was still coming down thickly.

White! The trees bore blankets on every branch, and stood in bare and dry circles. Beyond them lay an unbroken carpet, but perforated where grass stems protruded, each in a tiny tube, a hole in the snow, perhaps melted by the residual heat of the stem. The road could be discerned, when I looked closely enough, for the snow there was only an inch or two thick, much thinner than elsewhere. Here and there was a spot of color, a wildflower obstinately denying that there was any snow. Of wind, there was none. Snowflakes drifted straight down, a slow plummet, for each flake was large and fluffy. Sound was also absent; not a chirp of bird, nor a whisper of wind. Silence, clean white silence. Not only are the normal sounds of the forest, of the birds and insects and squirrels, not being created, but the aerial flakes soften, cushion, absorb any sounds there may be. Even the background tinkling of the flowing waters is suppressed before it can reach as far as an ear. It is a silence that forces one to listen, to strain for the slightest sound. You cannot help it, you *must* listen, for you are so certain there just *has* to be a sound. And there is. It is almost not there, but it is. The snow itself, each individual flake, makes a sound when impacting the ground, the crack of microscopic crystals breaking, shattering beneath their own weight. The sound is tiny, miniscule, too soft to detect, by itself. But there are millions of flakes, and millions of snaps, each bouncing, echoing from those crystals still falling. If you listen, listen *hard*, you just might hear them. But it is all you will hear.

My footsteps are relative roars as I carry my chair to a low mound in the snow. The tarp crackles and the snow chuffs when I uncover my nascent fire. A tiny touch of flame into the tinder rapidly grows, and flames leap several feet into the air, lapping at snowflakes like fish snapping up insects above a lake. The initial inferno swiftly subsides into a warm and constant glow, hissing and spitting as suicidal snow dissolves in the flames. Soon my eggs are sizzling in the pan, sprinkled with pepper, and peppered with snowflakes.

After breakfast, I sit in an oasis of warmth centered on my fire. The number of falling flakes diminishes, as if the fire has frightened them. Fewer and fewer, the flurries dwindle down to nothing. The gray sky swiftly lightens, and branches of blue form and widen. Streaks of sunlight break through, making the world explodes in brightness, in tiny rainbows and sparks of spectral color that merge into a blinding white glare, drowning out the glow of the fire, brightening the firs to a shrill green. The silence draws in on itself, beaten and broken by spattering drops as snow lading the branches melts and flees the heat of the sunlight, cowering into the moist shade around the trunks. Soon the sound is as that of a steady drizzle. The clouds are gone, but their snow has become rain, a long time delayed in its falling, but achieving its end, in the end. Warm wind stirs the air. Great slabs of snow slide from the trees, slushing to the meadow. Stalks of grass, bent and held down by their frozen burden, shake themselves free and draw themselves erect. The brook grows noisy, and not simply because the sounds are no longer blanketed, its level rising visibly as snowmelt swells into a torrent. The road transforms to a field of mud, which drains and dries even as I watch. Green patches form in the white, and grow, and merge, and soon the field is white patches in the green, white patches that shrink and sprout holes, patches that soon cease to shrink, and simple evaporate, fade away. A light, vague mist appears, then dissipates as fast as it formed.

By midafternoon, the last of the snow is gone. July has returned. The mountains are like that. Sometimes.

Rain Last Night

There was rain last night. Only a touch of light sprinkling, not enough to pay any mind, danced about shortly after noon, then gave up and went home. A bit more showed up in the mid-afternoon, and chased away a few city-folk, who hadn't enough sense to go out in the rain. We played tag for a while, the rain and I, till he got bored and wandered off. Then the big brother arrived. He was not playing; he had serious work to do, for the forest was dry, and the streams were low. It started with a light spatter, and steadily warmed up to a constant fall of big drops. I lounged under a thick tree, basking in the moist air, hearing the raindrops drowning out all other sounds, watching the duff slowly darken till it was time to light the cook fire. From the woodpile under a sheltering tarp, a handful of pine needles and a handful of twigs soon ignited a tepee of branches and small logs, and a bright blaze ignored the rain, boiling a pot of water as I watched from a dry seat under a lean-to. Eating a hot dinner in cool, dry comfort, I watched as the flames slowly succumbed to the rain, and listened to the sighing patter high in the trees. The birds were silent.

As the last light faded and the last ember dimmed, I retired to my tent, to snuggle in dry warmth and listen to the gentle, steady rhythm on the rain fly. Not the sharp stacatto of rain on a hard, stiff tin roof, but a lighter, less abrupt tapping, the sound stretched and softened by the yielding fabric. Nature's lullaby, like the murmuring almost-voices of a pebbled brook, slowly, gently, secretly leading the way to sleep.

The rain continued, steady, unchanging.

The first light of dawn caresses my face, and I awake to pure silence. I step out into dimness, a slightly vague light, relishing the chill quiet. There are no sounds at all, not even a dripping from the high limbs of the still-sleeping trees. A soft, distant chirp is followed, reluctantly but hopefully, by a second and, tentatively, a third. With an almost uncanny suddenness, the air brightens and comes into focus, and a

burst of happy chirps and trills shimmers through the air, their sweetness accented by the occasional discord of a raven. As the cloudless sky begins to glow, squirrels chitter and squabble on their branches. Day brightens as diamonds dance on the tall grass and a doe with her young one, barely more than a fawn, timidly emerges from nowhere. The sun is still hidden, but the tallest trees are crowned with gold. Far to the south, boils of clouds covertly rise. Later there will again be rain, and that is good. But for now, the world is perfect.

Dismal Morning

Dismal. Dreary. Dank. Damp. Dark. Chill. These are bad things. They are not desirable, not things to be sought, things to be created. They are to be avoided, they are ills to be cured. Anyone can tell you that. But are they correct?

I went to bed last night, tired after a long eight-hour ride, elevated from hours of drifting among sharp stars in a clear cold sky. Lulled to sleep by the murmuring chuckle of the nearby creek, I was wakened at three AM by a new sound, the patter of rain on the roof of my tent. It varied, stronger, lighter, there, gone, back. The sound was cold and wet, but I was warm and dry, and that made the cold and wet good. To lie in soft, warm comfort while breathing cold, almost icy air is, to me, the finest way to sleep. But I slept no more. To listen to the rain was of greater interest, of more fun, than to sleep.

In time, the first light appeared, and there was a dawn with no sunrise, for the sky was a uniform unbroken gray. I arose, dressed appropriately, and went out to wander in the wet. Yes, I am peculiar that way. Others like to walk in the sun, to feel the loving caress of warm light and warm wind. I like that too, but while some folks scamper to shelter at the first touch of a raindrop, and hunch shoulders and tightly squint eyes in their grimacing faces when forced to flee across forty feet of light dampness, I welcome the rain. In waterproof clothing, why should I fear it? Instead, I accept it, I cherish it, and then, no longer resisting, I can see it, know it, for what it is.

As the light brightens, everything grows clearer. The blurred and soft-focused masses of pre-dawn emerge as clear and sharp shapes, shapes which soften and blur again with distance. Only that which is close at hand is hard, solid, real. The farther away a thing lies, the less certain it is, the less likely. The tree beside me is clearly a pine. Those a distance off may also be pines. Then again, they may be fir, or spruce, or possibly even juniper. And the ones far away, well, they are trees. Though some of them may be a cliff of dark rock. Or maybe nothing, only shadows. It is difficult to be certain, or even to care. The shadowy shapes may be anything, Even fantasy. They may be trees, but moving, walking trees. The only way to be sure is to walk over there yourself. And by the time you get there, the trees you have left behind might be capering about, making faces behind your back. But even without the fantasy, the semi-blurred, semi-concealed shapes bear a singular beauty not seen in sharp sunlight. Not a better beauty or a lesser, but different, worthwhile in its own right.

And that is only the light. The sounds are also different. The ever-present patter and drip forms a different background which alters the forest melody. The same song, but the beat is Buddy Rich instead of Ringo Starr, or Karen Carpenter. "Fly Me to the Moon" by Frank Sinatra as opposed to Perry Como. The voice of the creek is lower, softer than the sparkling chatter in sharp sunlight. Your own footsteps are more yielding, less crunchy. The brushing of leaves against your clothes is now accompanied by the liquid tinkle of silvery bells. The surface of a normally silent pool hisses. It is a different world, made different by its saturation with water, and all of the effects the rain brings with it, but also made different by your attitude toward it, as a naked body is pornography or art, in a movie or a sculpture. It depends entirely on how you *choose* to view it.

Most people view rain, *choose* to view rain, as unpleasant. Have you never walked nude, or nearly so, in a warm tropical shower, or in a sudden downpour in a hot desert? Have you never stood in a waterfall? Have you never taken a shower, hot or cold? What, then, is so inherently bad about rain? Walk in it. If it is cold rain, wear waterproof clothing, but *walk* in it.

This morning is dark and drear, even dismal. But it is a *good* dismal. It counterpoints by contrast the bright and sunny mornings. It shows the true shapes of rocks, and of the foliage under trees, not hidden by deep and dark shadows cast by bright sun. It is also an admonishment. I had planned to ride into town today, to revisit favored scenes, and to get groceries. But nature is telling me to relax, to rest. I have come so far simply to enjoy this place. Enjoy it, then. Be a part of this environment during this day, during this long, soaking rain. This rain, and others like it, are the reason the flora is so green. The lushness it brings is the reason there are more animals, for the lushness is their food. I will be a part of this environment during days of dryness and warmth as well as during days of wetness and chill. To know one and not the other would be exactly like reading only every other page of a book. Sit in dryness and warmth in the rain, as in shade and cool in the sun. Wear raincoats in rain, and wide hats in sun. They are both real, and as comfortable as you make them. Or as dismal, dreary, and miserable. As *you* make them.

Drizzle

The overcast is solid, complete, though not uniform, for the thunderheads bull their way through like icebergs through broken pack ice, dark masses amongst lighter shades of gray. Random flashes followed by sharp cracks and slow grumbles continue the simile to floating glaciers and floes that fragment and grind each other to slush. For the edge of the icepack is never silent, and speaks in a voice remarkably similar to distant thunder, and sometimes not so distant.

The thunderstorms bypass my camp, riding on the ridges to the East and the West. Their waters wash the cliffs, carving intricate details into the ancient castles and battlements hewn from the soft rock. The topmost layer is hard, unyielding, almost impervious to the picks of ice and the battering rams of rain. Almost impervious, but not quite. The storms have sent their rain to run as streams, miners to undermine the mountain's curtain wall and open breaches in the defenses. And when the cliff falls away, cracks open in the capstone, cracks that allow a trickle of water to seep through, to wear the rubble within, to carve vertical gullies in the sheer face, deep gullies that reveal towers and turrets and keeps crowned by broken embrasures. They are called Castle Rocks, and their naming required as little imagination as the naming of Newfoundland.

Still, in the absence of thundershowers, there is some small rain in the valley, light, inconstant, a desultory drizzle. It is too much to allow the reading of a book, but not enough to deter a fire. The birds do not like it. As for me, I am not like the city-folks; I have enough sense to go out in the rain. My hat is waterproof, as are my coat and boots. My jeans are not, but there is wool beneath them, and the air is not cold. Besides, cold legs are of little moment. Ask any woman.

These woods are magical in the rain. The leaves perform their normal wind dances, fluttering and twisting in the breeze. Larger drops pull tiny columns of water up from the stream, but the rain avoids the trees, falling only in the meadows and the clearings, wetting only the helpless grasses and the trunks of fallen snags, leafless and unable to protect themselves. For the living leaves defend the dry trunks. Try as it might, the rain can find no entry. Every drop finds it's path occupied by a stalwart leaf, a shield that batters and shatters each assailant into a thin mist that can only drift gently down, dampening the waiting duff. As I drift through the dimness, only a drop now or two then strikes my armor and rebounds, often unnoticed.

My attention is mostly on the castles, slowly deepening in shade and blending to another hue. For a rock which is beige when dry may be pink when damp and red when wet. Others drench from tan to black, or from pale to pure white. Cracks worn by water-flows seem almost invisible when dry, except when emphasized by shadows, but stand stark when soaked by the runoff, while the bastions between them are still sheltered from the rain. And there a broad, flat, seemingly smooth slab of white stone receives the drizzle on unseen irregularities, and the eyebrows darken over sheltered eye-sockets, and the bridge of the nose becomes prominent, and the gray beard grows beneath, so that now, as at no other time, you can clearly see the Face of the Cliff.

The drizzle thickens, and the leaves begin to speak. "Hush, hush", they say, like a mother soothing her crying babe. The surface of the stream leaps jouyously to greet it's father from the sky. "Pa-pa", it says. "Pa-pa-pa-pa." The grass is silent, but it trembles and flinches at each new blow from above. The duff only darkens and drinks, insatiable, but the bare ground has had enough. It has filled it's cracks and dampened it's dust and refuses to accept any more. Puddles form, and trickles. No, not trickles, for that implies a continuous motion, and there is not enough water to flow. Say, rather, an enormous drop (enormous by the standards of a drop) forms upon the ground, and when it is large enough, surges forth an inch or three, then pauses to gather it's strength to surge again.

I stand beside a stately juniper, one whose thick foliage stubbornly refuses to admit the presence of rain. Even the dusty berries still appear to bear a coating of flour. No, the mulish juniper will continue to deny the rain. That is fine with me, for I can remain quite dry in it's presence. Even the mist of shattered raindrops is excluded from this haven of dryness.

The rain slackens a bit. It has never been heavy, not in the slightest degree, but it has been steady, continuous, and has now thoroughly soaked most of the flora. The small fauna, the rabbits and squirrels especially, are snug in their holes, nibbling stored food as they dimly remember the Outside being not wet. Now all of the scents of the forest are awakened, tiny particles pounded from their places by the impacts of the rain, carried through the air to be detected and admired. This is what people call the smell of rain, but the rain, of itself, owns no aroma at all. The smell of rain is the smell of rain-washed ... *everything*. And everything is here, here in the rain. Anything that is not here does not exist, not now, not here. Perhaps it will exist tomorrow. It does not matter. This is a unique world, the world of rain. It is different, it is itself. Is it better? Yes, of course, and no, definitely not! There is so much good in the worst, and so much bad in the best, that you might just as well stop labelling. Do not ignore the bad; that would be foolish, and possibly fatal. But do not ignore the good, because that, too, would be foolish, and possibly just as fatal. Take a walk in the rain. Seek out the good in it. There is a great deal to be found, and you might even find yourself. In the rain.

Thunderstorm

The storm is raging, and "rage" is the right word. Lightning is falling, north, south, west, and east, every minute, without fail, another bolt, or two, or three. Some are as close as a mile near, others three, five, eight miles, more. The storm is at least thirty miles wide, gigantic, monolithic, not a mass of thunderheads, but one gargantuan sprawling cloud. The forest has been sere, a desert for so long. The Forest Service has been battling at least six fires in the region, some disastrously large. Lightning has been the bogey, the ogre, the monster threatening to devour every tree in three great forests. And now it has come in force, the demon of the skies, flames from above, scores, hundreds, thousands of strikes, and no one has any idea how long the assault will prolong.

But there is hope, and more than just a ray. Say rather, a deluge of hope, for this is no dry storm. It has brought the Rain. And such rain! I have seen such intensity in a desert cloudburst, but that lasted only four or five minutes. This has continued for over an hour. The duff is soaked, the bare rocks gleam, the branches droop beneath the weight of water. Dry creek beds lie drowned by splashing streams. Flash floods roar through stone gullies. The incessant rain threatens to pummel the earth for hours more. . .

And then it slacks off. The northern sky turns blue, the western sky red. The rain eases, tapers, renews in momentary bursts, dwindles, dawdles, dies. Thunder rumbles only in the South, dimming in the distance, a fading tattoo. New-born pools seep slowly into the soil. Trees shake lingering drops from their limbs. Darkness falls as the light leaves in seeming sympathy to the retreating storm. And it is all over. For now.

The sky is almost clear when I slide into my sleeping bag. I would watch the stars, but it has been a long day, and I am tired. I fall asleep quickly, I know not for how long. A sudden sound wakes me. The rain has returned, a light, diminishing drumming above me, that slowly subsides as I drift back into sleep. I jolt awake to silence, with no idea why. I will sleep through almost anything, as long as it is normal and not very interesting. The unexplained will alert me in an instant. But now there is nothing, no sound or memory of sound, only deep darkness and total silence. Then thunder, as loud as a strike a half mile away, but not sudden, a casual grumble like the growl of a dog warning you to come no closer. Ah! A burst of light as bright as day to my night-adapted eyes, followed in a few more seconds by the sound of God's robe being torn in half. It is the cloud lightning, bolts leaping from one cloud to another, never nearing the ground, accompanied by no rain. Swift flashes and rumbles persist for some minutes. I know them now, I know there is no danger. I slip away once more as the aerial light show carries on. Suddenly I am awake, with no recall at all of awakening, an enduring roar dinning at my ears. Flash after brilliant flash, each followed within a second by an abrupt impact of white noise. This is Danger! This is heavy lightning tearing the trees within mere hundreds of feet. There are many tall pines, sixty, eighty, a hundred feet from me. I *should* be safe from strikes and even from flying branches or toppling trees. Should be. There is never a guarantee. A last flash, then several more claps with no preceeding bolt, and I realize the danger was illusory; the barrage was a mile or two away, and the sounds only overlapped, producing a seeming of nearness. A few more lingering lights, some tarrying thunder. I sleep.

When next I waken, it is quiet, and slightly light. I step outside to relieve myself. It is four AM, more or less, and just dawn, the first tentative tweets of frightened birds breaking the silence and breaking the day. The air is clean, the sky is clear, the last stars fading, the crescent moon sliding down. And it is cold, not fifty degrees, a wonderful contrast to the summer heat I have just left behind. I listen to an elk greeting the day, and go back to bed.

Now it is the Morning After. The sun is well risen, and I gratefully absorb its warmth. A fair wind, fifteen miles per hour, blows from the South. Aspen leaves flitter and flutter, flashing dark green/light green, faster than I can blink my eyes, much faster. Why do they do this? How does it enhance their survival? Does it break the force of the wind, dissipating its energies? Does it pump sap through the twigs? Or is it just fun? The trees decline to tell me. Another elk bugles nearby. Perhaps the meadow will be their lists, perhaps they will hold a tourney and I will watch their jousts. I must remember to keep my camera handy. A coyote howls in the far distance. A closer one replies. They speak a few sentences, then fall mute. Pines whisper. Aspens chatter. The birds are mostly silent, intent on nabbing insect entrees driven out of hiding by the wetness. For all is wet. Soaked. The ground is squishy with water working its way to the water table far below. It has only managed a bit more than an inch of its journey so far, and so far more to go. The wind knocks drops off of the taller grass, and flings tiny droplets from the pine needles. The aspen are already dry; perhaps that is why they shivver, like a dog fresh from a good drench. A chipmunk ventures forth for seeds, till a swooping hawk sends him scurrying for safety, a sanctuary achieved by a bare foot. The hawk reverses his dive and resumes his soaring sentry-go. Breakfast will be a bit late.

A high haze is forming, cirrus hints of things to come. The northern sky is cerean blue, no warnings, no omens, nothing to say about the course of the day. But to the South, a curtain of cumulus rises ominously. The morning is beautiful, a fine time for any activity I choose. I had better enjoy it, for I know it will soon slip away. Yesterday's storm was a harbinger. The Monsoon is coming. It is time to go.

A New Story

A true adventure is never fun when it happens, except to a fool (well, to someone more foolish than I am). It is only enjoyable afterwards, when the danger is past, and one can tell the tale.

Some people seek tales of adventure. You will find very little in my works, because I seek to avoid it. The classic definition of adventure is "Someone else having a hard time a long way away". Even so, adventure sometimes catches up to me.

I had spent the Spring in New Mexico, mostly. Clement temperatures, beautiful landscapes, plenty of wildlife, good friends, hot showers and electricity in the State Parks. But this year was dry, very dry. The entire state was suffering extreme fire danger, or worse (yes, there *is* a stage beyond Extreme). I was chased out of one park because it was threatened by a wildfire, and denied access to a couple of others because of the hazard. In fact, the entire Santa Fe National Forest, and all State Parks within it, were closed to all public access, except driving through on established highways. But being evacuated from a campground, though not pleasant, does not qualify as adventure. Not unless you are striving to outrun a fire.

Summer arrived, and I could be reasonably sure there would be no snow in the mountains, so it was time to move north. I planned a two-stage run to the Black Hills, with an overnight stop in a motel, by way of Kansas. Why Kansas? Because I had never biked there. Been there, but only in a car. Not in the wide open, exposed to the elements, which is one of the best aspects of biking. Also, as it turned out, one of the worst. Adventurous. First there was a headwind, which makes bike handling a chore, especially when it is partly a crosswind. The bike is not exactly tossed around, but there is a definite pressure, on one side or the other, which means one hand has to push on the handle grip while the other hand pulls. And the pressure is not steady, rather more of a series of weak but sharp jerks. Holding a bike on a straight and smooth course is work, and it is wearing. Plus, the fact that the wind is mostly headwind means it requires more power to move it, and that means lower gas mileage; instead of my usual thirty-eight or forty, I was reduced to less than twenty-seven! Thus more frequent stops for fuel.

Still, the countryside was beautiful. Almost from the moment I entered Kansas, the land was more green, almost dramatically so. It was much like western Nebraska, except that Nebraska was mostly pasturage and Kansas was mostly cropland. There is pasture in Kansas; there were several places that reminded me of the dairy land around Oasis Park in New Mexico: Cattle feed lots, smelling strongly of ammonia and cow manure. Mostly, though, it was wheat, and a bit of maize. And swamps. Oh, yes, swamps in Kansas. Not permanent. At first I thought they were ponds, but on closer look, they were flooded fields. It was rather intriguing to me, having just come from New Mexico, where a quarter inch of rain in twelve hours is a welcome blessing, a good, solid rain. (If this tale had a soundtrack, you would now be hearing a premonitory rumble. The laughter of the Gods.) Shortly I stopped to refuel. Just pouring gas from a can into the bike's tank. As I finished, a local farmer came by and chatted about (naturally) the weather. Seems they just had a storm the previous afternoon, which dumped more then two inches of rain and a fair bit of hail; he was concerned about hail damage to his wheat, which was less than two weeks from harvest. Two inches in just over an hour! And it was the third such fall in the last ten days. And there was a fair chance of another this afternoon. I was bemused, but not concerned (ominous rumble). The skies of the North were clear, and that is where I was bound.

I continued, another hundred miles or so to the town of Goodland (imaginative names around here), where I filled my gas tanks. Goodland is right on an Interstate highway, so there are several motels. It is a good place to stop for the night, but I could still get in another three or four hours on the Road. I continued north. Thirty-some miles took me to the next town, or village, where I stopped to watch the clouds. Thunderheads. Fast moving, northeast to southwest. Right across my route. No motels here. Seven miles west lay another town, again with poor chances of a motel. Decisions. Push on in the hope of finding shelter, or backtrack to Goodland. I do not like to backtrack. If I do, I will not have time to visit the Black Hills and still make my reservation at Owen Creek. Two big black clouds ahead. If I wait a few minutes, I can dash between them and miss the rain. Beyond them there is a solid white overcast, nothing dark and threatening. I am a pretty good judge of weather, having a great deal of experience with it. Mountain weather. Desert weather. Not Kansas flatlands weather. I chose to go for it. I aimed straight for the hole and dashed through to the other side, safe and dry.

Arrogance goes before destruction, and a haughty mind precedes a fall. The solid white overcast on the other side was not overcast. It was rain. Not sheets of rain. Solid. The great Kansas Cloudburst. I watched a few waves sweeping along the highway ahead, but moving northwest to southeast, exactly perpendicular to the thunderheads' motion. I pulled over at a level place just off the road. The road ahead disappeared, there was no shelter in sight, and no time to turn around. I made sure my gear was tight, ducked my head, and started to drown. I have been in a Kansas Cloudburst before. In a car. Rain so intense you could not make out the front of the hood. Water that stood half an inch deep on the windshield, and who knows how deep on the hood itself. This time I was sitting on a bike. Exposed to the elements. I was wearing a bison hide jacket and chaps, which I had designed and made myself, and had waterproofed with beeswax cream. They are close fitting at neck and wrists, covering all but head, hands, feet and crotch. No water penetrated them, but some seeped under the collar, not much, only a tiny percentage. But what is a tiny percentage of the Pacific Ocean? My gloves were not waterproof, nor was I wearing my waterproof boots. It did not matter, for the rain would have seeped past the ankles and wrists. I was, after all, virtually under water. I could not see the far side of the road; I could barely see the *near* side, a good three feet away! Now and then a pickup would go by, fifteen, twenty miles per hour. Locals, perhaps, who knew the road cold, and knew how to maneuver through the weather. Or maybe tourists, travelers, unimaginative fools who had no idea what they were risking.

The rain slacked off. I could now see thirty or forty feet. Decisions. Creep forward in hopes of a motel? Turn back to the last village and beg shelter from someone? Or retreat to Goodland and a motel?

I turned back. At the turn south, I pulled up in the lee of a wall and looked around. As the sadistic Gods arranged it, this was the wall of a diner. A classic country diner, with signs promoting good, solid country fare. Biscuits and gravy! I *love* biscuits and gravy! In a warm, dry, out-of-the-wind diner. Which, this being Sunday, was closed.

The rain stopped. Pretty much. I could see there were waves wearing their way south at about forty miles per hour. I could go south at forty miles an hour, too. I could stay between the rain-waves, more or less, and reach a motel. Thirty miles. Forty-five minutes. It was doable, and I had a brand-new front tire with deep tread, so riding in the rain is not the hazard non-bikers think it is. I started the motor and set out.

The plan worked well. I flew through a constant drizzle, and could have done sixty, except then I would catch up with the rain and have to slow down to twenty, or ten, or zero. The water continued to seep down my neck, annoying, but not really uncomfortable. I had made about ten miles when conditions changed again. The rain ahead and the rain behind converged, and I had to slow. The temperature dropped, and dropped again. I began to hear a pinging on my helmet, as the rain became intermixed with hail. The seepage became chill. What little rain worked its way under my visor drenched my moustache and beard. Licking it off was like drinking from a glass, and this was only minor leakage! If I had had no visor, I expect I would have had difficulty breathing. I was barely doing ten, and considering stopping, but there was not even a tree for shelter (this *is* Kansas, after all). And that is when the Adventure began.

What, you say, this is not already having a hard time? Nope. Hard enough, not pleasant, but I am still warm, and though it might take another hour or so, there is no reason I cannot reach a haven. Adventure, true adventure, requires danger, requires risk, a distinct chance of never being able to tell anyone about it. To qualify as an Adventure, this scenario requires something more, something like, oh, say, lightning.

The first bolt was at least three miles away. Or maybe the rain was just so loud it drowned out the thunder. I could not actually see the bolts through the dense rain, but there was an unmistakeable lightness, a sort of yellowing of the gray-white rain. They became brighter and more frequent, and soon I could hear them. Then I *could* see them, blurred and distorted, but bright enough to penetrate a half mile. Then less.

Now, most of you probably know what to do when caught in a lightning storm. Go to the middle of a large field, away from any trees or utility poles, and lie down. But not in water; stay away from streams and ponds. Do not be the tallest object in the vicinity. Well, I was in the middle of a large field, called Kansas. It was also a pond, if not of standing water, then at least just as saturated as it could possibly be. The road itself was a stream. And as to being the tallest object, why, even if I lay down, there would still be nothing taller. On the bike, in motion, I would at least be on rubber tires. Wet ones. And the rain was changing to hail, and I was getting wet in spite of waterproof gear. My hands, feet and crotch were already as soaked, as saturated as they could get. And cold. So I had a choice: Stop, lie down, and risk hypothermia, possibly for hours, or ride and find shelter in less than an hour, at the risk of pulling down a bolt of lightning.

I may be a fool, I may be crazy, but I am not stupid. I rode. Lightning continued to fall, more frequently. At least three times a bolt struck within a thousand feet. I had been in a boat that was lightning-struck in the Caribbean; I remembered the sizzling hum that preceded the bolt. If anything like that started, I was ready to drop the bike and roll away. But it was not necessary. The closest call came as I passed a Wal-Mart, five or six hundred feet away. It was struck. I saw it, heard it, felt it. But just beyond, almost next door, was a motel. I was back in Goodland.

And then the real storm arrived.

I checked in, got a room, and carried my essential gear to it. I have a pair of 20MM ammunition cans for saddlebags. Tough, solid steel, and utterly waterproof. That is where I carry my clothes. I immediately took a long hot shower. I have learned, in the Wilds, that cold is not really dangerous, and wet is at worst an uncomfortable annoyance. Cold *and* wet, together, though, that can easily kill you. Thus my first concern was to get warm, then get in dry clothes. I did not catch pneumonia. Didn't even get a sniffle or scratchy throat. Had a good hot meal and a long night's sleep, then resumed my journey in the early morn. I was lucky.

I am afraid the farmers were not so lucky. For twenty miles along the road I saw banks of hail, some of them as much as two feet deep. Fields of golden wheat in the last stages of ripening bore wide swaths of flattened stalks. I do not know how widespread this destruction was, but in the area which I traversed, at least a quarter of the wheat crop was lost. I feel for the farmers, I sympathize with their loss, but I also see what might have been for me, if I had been just one hour more in the storm. I have seen pickup trucks, four-wheel drive, trying to drive on a hail-covered road; they only spun their wheels. On a motorcycle, it would have been worse. Perhaps a Motocross master could manage to keep a bike upright under such bad conditions; I could not. I might have been lying by the side of the road, fallen where the cold had overcome me in a desperate attempt to hike to town after abandoning an unusable bike. I might have succeeded. Maybe.

I hope you enjoyed this adventure. *I* did not! But I will still travel in Kansas, and other Plains states. I will pay a bit more attention to the weather, and seek shelter sooner, if it should seem necessary. For it all turned out well, and, after all, I do have a new story to tell!

Not an Adventure

It has been an interesting year, between fire and water. Not a single major plan survived them, and most changed several times. My major route changed between Washington and Wisconsin, though mostly in Wyoming, and every change was dictated by Fire. More precisely, by smoke. I was kicked out of one campground, and barred from several others, not by any act of my own, but by the threat of forest fires. Seems the Authorities feared I might get killed by a fire, then sue them. But I did not see a single wildfire, did not even get within ten miles of one, though I did get to watch the smoke columns of a couple. And later, smoke from distant fires so degraded local conditions, I pulled up stakes and went elsewhere. "Distant", in this case, means hundreds of miles and two or three states away. It could be blamed on weather. Some areas had a wet Winter, and the extra water resulted in enormous growth of brush, which, as it often does, burned at the end of Summer. Other areas had a very dry Winter, so the existing brush was tinder-dry and almost explosively ready to burn. And it did.

Weather was also responsible for the Water. From a drenching Kansas Cloudburst that washed away one plan, to a long drizzle that persuaded me to stick around a few additional days rather than ride in it, rain has affected me more this year than in any other.

I left my last campsite just ahead of the rain. The forecast said it would start by late morning, but it was just starting to spit at eight AM when I set out. It followed me for more than three hundred miles as I headed south, mostly clear skies ahead, but deep gray, even black, always in persistant pursuit. I sat through two long delays while road repair crews limited traffic, and lost half an hour. It was not enough to allow the storms to catch up, but it was sufficient to set up the ambush. But I did not know about that, so I sat through the delays cheerfully. I always enjoy chatting with the flagman; his (or, increasingly commonly, her) job must be tediously boring. Plus, I welcome a chance to dismount and stretch my legs, and take a long look at the countryside, whatever it may be. Pardon? The ambush? Oh, yes, that was set for my arrival.

I turned off the highway for the six-mile ride to Brantley Lake, and saw that what had been drifting along far to one side was now looming dead ahead, and approaching swiftly. It was another of those gray-black clouds, but not one that had been following me. No, this one was home-grown, just waiting for me, and was trailing a dense mass of rain-lines. Here in the Southwest, such lines are often seen, but usually terminate well above the ground, as the frightfully arid air absorbs the drops soon after they begin their descent. Not these. They reached all of the way to the ground, and left it dark and sodden. Still, this one looked like it would pass a mile or so to my left. That is also quite common out here, to stand in bright, hot sunlight, while watching a squall utterly soak the ground less than a mile away. But I did not realize that the road I was on made a dog-leg to the left, just a mile or so short of the campground.

I almost made it. Only a single mile of road still lay ahead when the first drops fell upon me. I had little choice but to ride into it, which was no hardship, as my riding gear is waterproof, and my bags and stowage are water-tight. But by the time I entered the campground proper, the downfall was a torrent. The in-camp speed limit was ten MPH, which was also the fastest I could safely go in such an intense rain. I reached my campsite, dismounted, and took shelter in the ramada. And there I stayed for the next half hour, waiting till the rain had stopped and even the denoument of drizzle had dwindled to almost nothing. Only then did I unpack and pitch the tent.

While I waited, I thought about the road-repair delays, and blessed them. Yes, I was grateful for them, because had they not occured, I would have reached the campsite, contemplated the oncoming cloud, and chosen to race it. I would have doffed my heavy (and waterproof) bison-hide coat and chaps, cleaned the rocks from the site, unpacked the tent and spread it, and been setting the stakes preparatory to raising it, when the rain would have struck. Then I would stubbornly rush to get the poles up and guys adjusted, and swiftly been soaked through. Arriving in the rain was much preferable.

That was the last rain I saw. For the rest of my stay, there were few clouds, and the temperature rose every day, the last two days well into the nineties. But yesterday the weather forecast called for a rainy night followed by a very rainy day. Worse, the route I would take today was expected to have even heavier rain. Several groups are pulling out right now. One couple has told me they are leaving two days earlier than they had planned. Why? Because it is raining. The weatherman says it is going to rain all day. They are *taking advantage* of the rain! Normally, the rain would ruin their day. They could not go boating, they could not go hiking, they could not ride their bicycles. They would get wet. I do not know. I have never gone boating and *not* gotten wet. I like hiking in the rain. It is also a lot cooler, which is much more conducive to physical activity than ninety-degree heat. But they would rather drive through the rain, warm and dry in the cab of their truck. As for me, I prefer to stay off of the wet roads, especially knowing that most drivers cannot handle them.

Now, I can ride in the rain. I have the skills and the gear. What I do not have is the desire. The following day is forecast to be clear and cool, ideal bike weather. I have a reservation at the next campground, but I can arrive a day late. So I shall just sit this out. It only costs me an extra four bucks. And while I dislike riding in the rain, I love sitting snug in a warm and dry tent, feeling smugly secure against the cold and clammy damp, listening to the musical rooftop patter and watching the drifting rainlines come and go.

Some people actively seek discomfort and danger; they call it Adventure. Some people are fools.

Sky

Nightfall

The sun is going down, drifting to the mountains. The shadows are long, trunks of trees drawing irregularly spaced parallel bars across the duff. The trees are tall pillars, bereft of branches for forty feet; the sun is below the branches, so the world is entirely banded with light and shadow. A flashback of the past presents a dichotomy of then and now.

Then was the City. The background was the constant rumble of motors, punctuated by a frequent horn or an insufficiently rare siren. It was a never-ending drone that you soon ceased to hear. The air carried a light tinge of almost-yellow, invisible in the light, save for the bit of blur that smudged everything. Office buildings, apartment houses, parking structures loomed as artificial hills, cliffs for the pigeons, lining the valleys of avenue and boulevard. Trees stood in straight rows on the concrete banks of the tar street streams. Rectilinear meadows surrounded the foothill arrays of houses. The sun descended, casting squared shadows over acres of asphalt and cement. The West blazed red as sunlight refracted in the air itself, in the all but invisible haze that is normal for this place. The light faded, the sky darkened. The clouds lay upside down, lighted from below, darkest on top. A star appeared, and another; soon all twelve beamed through the blackness. On the ground, a constant twilight prevailed. The sounds of traffic persisted. The stunted night was as full as it could get. Barring the infrequent power failures, when the Wilds made a quick trip to the City. Apparantly the Wilds like to take the odd vacation, too.

Now is the Forest. It is quiet. No birds sing, no breeze whispers the trees, no squirrels complain. In the background, crickets begin to chorus their chirps. From far away comes a single short coyote yelp. In the near distance, sharp hatchet chops signal a camper belatedly preparing a fire. A child laughs. No doors slam. No motors growl. All else is still.

The air is clear. Everything is in sharp focus, unblurred, even the trees on the ridge a mile away. It grows cooler, slowly. The last rays of sunlight are warm on my skin. Wisps of white smoke rise through the branches, diffusing into blur and nothing. Light slowly climbs the trees, and shade floods the valley, filling the far side, flowing from the West. The sun touches the mountain, dwindles and disappears. A slight breeze brings a touch of pine; a straggler bee blunders homeward. In the tops of trees, sunlight begins to gather in groups that, one by one, leap into the sky. Birds chirp an evening song, calling the curfew, settling in to sleep. Only the tallest trees bear the blaze of day, swaying in the sunset wind, an erratic wind, stumbling and stopping, fading away, then flowing again. The last light rushes west, where the sky is a bright yellow that somehow skips green as it fades east and north to palest blue. There are no clouds to chase the sun and blaze in a hopeless quest to save the day. Birds finish their arias, and crickets resume the chorus. Shade claims the last forest spire, and the only remaining sign of wind is in the slight drift of smoke rising not quite straight. The last swallow darts across the sky, and the first bats follow, swooping and slipping, bouncing off of unseen obstacles in the air, animate pinballs swallowing a high score of gnats and mosquitoes, bless them! Yellow is dying. In the sky and in the leaves, it fades to pale orange. Leaves darken to brown, the sky to pink and purple. The sky above was blue before; now it has eased to a light gray, or a gray of light. A lonesome hawk drifts south, searching for a bedtime snack. The green of trees is becoming black. In its country way, the blackness starts in the West where the sky is still light; in the East, bark is still brown, needles are still green. A late squirrel sounds an angry alarm. Perhaps a predator threatens his tree. The note changes, sharpens, cuts short in a squeal. Perhaps he was trapped on the ground. Perhaps the hawk has found his snack.

The last of the western pink has become a dark white; the gray above darkens to blue. All of the trees are black, and shade descends to shadow. The blue above darkens back to gray. The whole horizon, lingering lighter than the zenith, fades at last. The darkening dome of gray deepens to an unblemished expanse of even dark, only slightly lighter in the lowest West. A sudden spark mars the perfection, a star that does not fade into visibility, but leaps to an instant glow as if created at just that moment. Another point appears, and another, rebels against the growing black, beacons of light, patriots rejecting the absolute dominion of dark. They will hold the high points, resolute warriors, till the moon rises.

The sky is not truly black; the trees are darker, their silhouettes clear and stark. The ground is invisible, or almost so. Subtle hints of rocks lie scattered about. Fallen pine cones are deeper dots. An owl calls, confusing its prey, patiently waiting for a mouse to panic and run from real safety to imagined sanctuary, and fall beneath the silent hunter. All of the sky is now dark, from horizon to horizon, uniform but for the stubborn stars. Even the Southwest is as dark as the rest. There lies the city, but it is far enough away; its loom is too weak to scale the hills.

Night is full.

Full Moon

Somewhere not too far away, a wildfire is blazing. It is far enough that the smoke clouds have dispersed into a uniform thin haze that softens and slightly blurs the cliff across the canyon, and dims and reddens the early morning and late afternoon sun. Right now, the morning after, the Sun is two hours above the horizon, and I can stare directly at it with no discomfort, and no after-image. The haze fairly ruins star-gazing. It is not enough to block most of the familiar stars, but the dimmer ones are not bright enough to pierce the haze. The grandeur simply never happens.

That did not matter last night, for it was the night of the Full Moon, and her dazzle would bedim and obscure the lesser stars in even the most pellucid sky. The haze would not cloud the Moon herself. Perhaps a bit of halo, a glory, might surround her, but the details of her face would not be smudged. But haze refracts the light and reveals the colors within. Red and orange are common; who has not seen a blood-red moon? But sometimes, rarely, very very rarely, we see the other end of the spectrum. Sometimes the Moon turns blue. This has been a truly celestial summer, with rare sights, almost once-in-a lifetime displays, becoming almost common. I am hoping for a super-nova, not too close. (If Vega died, so would we!) But they are too random, too rare, and utterly unpredictable. The last big one occurred a thousand years ago, and was visible even in the day. But a Blue Moon could happen, and it could very well happen tonight.

I usually have a fire in the morning, but this night, I lit one just before dark. I cooked my dinner, and watched the flames while I ate. It took a while for the Moon to climb over the eastern ridge, and by the time it did, the fire was mostly sullen coals, enough to warm me, but not enough to degrade my view of the night sky. The Moon rose in scarlet splendor, as red as I have ever seen her, swiftly soaring into a deep brown sky. Once well aloft, her rapid pace slowed, and the Moon appeared to gather energy, glowing more strongly, slowly segueing into a deep orange, brightening and fading into yellow, lighter, whiter, and . . . no more. She settled into a radiant, blemished white, slightly jaundiced by just a tinge of yellow, her light so intense it burned through the haze as if it was not there at all. But she went no further. She did not turn blue.

It was a disappointment, but not a great one. The odds were never large; it was only a possibility, a slim chance. It was fun to hope for. The consolation prize was generous: The entire face of the Moon lay spread before me. With braced binoculars, I drifted across the moonscape. The Sea of Tranquillity, where the Eagle landed, and all Mankind took a giant leap. Tycho Crater, whose long rays embrace the entire face, where an asteroid succeeded in shooting the moon, and almost split it into several smaller spheres. Close, but just a scar. The brightly glowing highlands, mountain ranges eroded only by a rain of rock. Dark seas, mares of magma spewed forth in the convulsions following some titanic cosmic catastrophe, long, long ago, when the Moon's core was still molten. And craters on craters on craters on craters, new ones forming every day, for the Moon receives as many meteors as the Earth, but hers do not burn away. They strike, every one, and every one produces a crater, mostly tiny, a few inches across, but some so big, their walls cannot be seen from their centers, since the walls lie beyond the horizon. Earth would look like this, were it not for the atmosphere that stops most impacts, and works to wash away the scars of the few that manage to get through.

Moonwatching is more interesting when the Moon is not full, for the terminator, the edge of light creeping across the land, casts long shadows, highlighting details, outlining outcroppings with shadows and sparks. But the Moon at full displays her entire face, and requires less magnification, indeed, none at all, to feel the glory and magnificence. Even the naked eye is sufficient to allow one to fall under the spell of Luna's Beauty.

As the Moon approached zenith, I said farewell. There will be no Blue Moon this summer, but there are four more chances this year. And there is next year, and the next. The Moon is not going away, and some day I will see her blue once again.

It is good to have something to look forward to.

Moonlight

Light is a wonderful thing, but how we react to it is more wonder full still. A well-lighted room seems as bright as broad daylight, as bright as a clear, sunny day, but in fact, the daylight is a hundred times as strong. The room just seems as bright because our eyes adapt to it, physically. The irises of our eyes open wide, and the pupil expands to a centimeter diameter, letting in a hundred times as much light as it does when strong light causes it to contract to a mere millimeter. And thus we can read in the dim artificial light, and we can still see colors.

There are two kinds of sensors in our eyes, rods and cones. The rods detect only light or dark, on or off. The cones sense colors, and require more energy, more light to react. And thus, when the light dims enough, the colors fade away, and all we can see are shades of gray. And that is why the stars, which come in many colors, all appear white, except the very brightest, and even then only to people with very sensitive eyes. Mars and Betelgeuse are red, Jupiter is orange, Vega is pale blue. But not to most people.

The moon itself appears slightly yellow, naturally, since that is the color of the sunlight it is reflecting, though the rocks and dust up there are actually a soft gray. Often the moonlight is red or orange, when the moon is rising or setting, and the light refracts on water or dust in the atmosphere, just as the sunlight can appear red when the sun is near the horizon. And rarely, very rarely, when atmospheric conditions are just right, the moon appears blue. This is the true Blue Moon. It is *not* the second full moon in a calendar month; that is a lie invented by some fool, probably perverting the language to use in some marketing campaign.

Moonlight is white, even when the moon is yellow, or red, or even blue. Why? Because it is too dim to trigger the color sense. Moonlight is white, and everything it illuminates is white, or gray, and everything not illuminated is black. The night world is a different world from that of the day. The rocks are different, featureless outlines, gray silhouettes, larger or smaller than they are during the day. Trees are amorphous, shapeless, and black, blacker than anything else, as if they are still absorbing every flicker of light that falls upon them. And the inhabitants of the night are a different population from those who wander the day. Just as the day is safe, familiar, friendly, and the night is sinister, strange, and dangerous, so it is with the animals. The diurnal roam the day; the nocturnal stalk the night.

Moonlight changes all of that. Masses of shadow become fields of grass, shapeless blurs re-form into trees. Rodents appear from nothing, and coyotes scramble to silhouette themselves against the moon. Ghosts and hoo-doos and bogies shrink into the shadows, and fairies dance in the moonbeams. Or they may be moths. Yes, probably moths. You have no idea how many moths teem in the night airs!

And a frost or heavy dew will enrich the sands and plains, covering them in diamonds that glitter and flash. Mists cloak the brush and half-hide their features like the sheer veils of an odalisque, concealing flaws and enticing imagination to enhance what may or may not be there. The desert, so blank and featureless in the day, becomes an enchanted kingdom by moonlight, mostly because so much is only half seen, and the mind must fill in the gaps. Even more so when scattered clouds drape the desert in mystery, mystery which only partly vanishes when the moonlight returns, as a breaking wave will completely submerge a rock, but leave the rock wet and gleaming when it re-emerges.

The desert moonlight has always seemed brighter than the moonlight anywhere else. Perhaps it is the pale color of the sands, reflecting more light to my eyes. Perhaps it is because I usually see deserts in Winter, when we are a few million miles closer to the sun. Whatever the reason, I have known times in the desert, when the moon was closest to Earth and at the full, when the light was enough to read by, and colors could be discerned, barely, almost vaguely, but definitely there.

Desert moonlight is beautiful. I was going to say it is among the best, but that is without meaning, for they all are. The moonpath on a still pond, or on a ruffled lake, is beautiful. So is moonlight on a broad, calm river, or on raging rapids. There is no sight quite like the moon on snow-capped peaks, or a set of tree-clad mountain ridges. Nothing is more beautiful than the snow-covered field, or the same field in Spring, or Summer, or Fall, when it is bathed by moonlight. A full moon setting over the ocean provides a trail of light the sun can never match. And the Grand Canyon by moonlight is even more spectacular, more grand than the same scene in the sun.

Comparisons do not exist. There is no "more" and no "less", no "better", no "best". Moonlight is beautiful, wherever it is, whenever it may be. Perhaps that is why cultures have moon goddesses, but never a moon god.

Moonshadow

In the Winter, when we are closest to the sun, the Moon shines at her brightest in the deep desert, where the air is clear and dry, and by midnight has usually become quite free of turbulence, and the stars shine brightly and steadily. But when the Moon is full, and especially when she is nearest to the Earth, the moonlight is at its brightest, strong enough to read by, almost intense enough to activate color vision. This is the best time of all to hike in the desert, when it is cool and bright. And this is when the Moon casts her best shadows.

Moonshadows are deeper, darker than sunshadows. There is less ambient light, less to reflect, to soften and dilute the almost utter blackness that lies beneath the plants and rocks. The little creatures of the night can scamper across shining sands, then abruptly vanish in the dark, utterly invisible even if they move, and they do not move, not even twitch, or blink.

Strictly speaking, though, these are not truly moon shadows; they are plantshadows and rockshadows, where objects have blocked the sunlight which has reflected off of the Moon. And they exist in the earthshadow, the great eight thousand mile wide shadow cast by our planet, the shadow that creates the night, and thus renders the other shadows possible. And when the Moon is absent from the sky, and the sky is free of clouds, and the land is free of light pollution, then we see the starshadows, faint, rarely noticed, scarcely even present. And in the sky, especially in the Milky Way in the wide skies of the West, we see the greatest shadows of all, the shadows of the immense dust clouds, shadows hundreds, thousands of light years across, blocking the light emanating from the core of the galaxy. Imagine it: A cloud of dust so huge, so thick, it can block out the light of an entire galaxy!

But it is one of the smaller shadows that is the most impressive, smaller than the Earth, larger than those of plants, and rocks, and even mountains. It is the moonshadow, the *true* moonshadow, a thousand miles across, rarely seen, only when the newest of new moons lies directly, exactly between the Sun and the Earth. And even then, it is only visible in a narrow band a couple of hundred miles across, and most of that is only partial shadow, enough to dim the sunlight, but not completely obscure it. Only in the smallest strip, less than a hundred miles wide, does the thousand-mile bulk of the Moon block out the entirety of the Sun and bring on a short, dramatic night. This is the Eclipse, the Total Eclipse of the Sun.

I had never seen the Total Eclipse. I have seen partials on several occasions, enough to darken the land, enough to bring on a dimness, a sort of twilight, but always a good ten percent of the Sun's face, maybe more, remained visible. Not today. Today is my first chance to see Totality. It will be an annular eclipse, meaning the Moon will appear just slightly smaller than the Sun, and a thin ring, the merest sliver, of the Sun will protrude. But it will be dark, dark enough that the totality may be verified safely by the naked eye. For three hours the spectacle will endure, from the first shadow of obscurement to the final escape of the golden orb. Ninety minutes of gradually fading light, two minutes of totality, then ninety more minutes of returning day.

I have been planning this day for six months. Being a full-time wanderer, I can go where I please. I chose a campground a hundred miles north, which meant a two-hundred-mile round trip on my bike. This was an added treat. Any excuse for a bike ride is a good one. There were several campgrounds right on the path of totality, but none were reservable; it would take sheer luck, and lots of it, to secure a site in one of them at the right time. I could have reserved a motel room along the path, just for a night or two, but I am very much averse to sleeping indoors. And besides, the price would be exorbitant, starting in the hundreds of dollars per night for reservations made long in advance, rising as The Day approached, and culminating at three thousand dollars per night in Casper, Wyoming, and at that, you had to take two nights each one at three thousand dollars. They may have been more expensive elsewhere. No, I preferred my plan.

I loaded my gear and set off at dawn for a leisurely ride to a good viewing spot. Ten miles north of Thermopolis, I entered the band of totality. The ideal locale would be just south of Shoshone, but I expected that area to be packed. A few miles south of Thermopolis, the traffic became thick. Thirty miles from Shoshone, and cars nearly bumper to bumper crawled at less than thirty miles per hour. With less than an hour to go before the eclipse began, they would never reach their destinations in time. A good open spot, safely off of the road, presented itself, and I took it. I would only have a single minute of totality instead of the two or more at the exact center of the path, and the annular ring might be just a hair lopsided, but it was quite sufficient. I set up and grabbed a sandwich, then settled down to enjoy the spectacle.

Half an hour later, the eclipse begins. Just the tiniest nibble out of the upper edge, unnoticeable without a good filter. For the next hour, the flaw in the sun slowly enlarges till a quarter of the disk simply is not there. So flexible are our eyes that no dimunition of the light is detectable. The air is warm, with no trace of a breeze, but that will change. The only clouds are near the horizon, and there is no slightest possibility of any atmospheric interference with the show. The traffic has dwindled to almost nothing.

The birds are unconcernedly going about their business, pursuing the equally oblivious insects. Grasshoppers chew blades, butterflies flit from flower to flower, and a small flock of sheep grazes as they always do. Two men argue over whether protective lenses are really needed after the eclipse has progressed to the point where the glare no longer obscures the shadow. One maintains that it cannot be so dangerous, or the Government would not allow eclipses to be held. Perhaps he thinks the Moon could be arrested. Or fined, and the proceeds used to finance the space program.

Half of the Sun is obscured. The pale light has become noticeably dimmer, and a cool breeze has arisen. The sheep do not notice (they hardly ever notice anything), the insects pay no apparant attention, but the birds seem hesitant.

Three-quarters dark. It is almost twilight. Almost. The light is odd. No, the *dark* is odd. Shadows lie under the trees, not beside them, and they are sharp and distinct as only midday shadows can be. The light level is that of an overcast day, but in such weather, there should *be* no shadows. And the air is cooling, as it should at dusk. But the Sun is still rising, still an hour and a half from zenith.

Ninety percent. The light is very dim, though ample for reading. The color is normal for noon, no reddening as is usual at sunset. None at all. The birds have begun flocking together, returning to their nests The butterflies have disappeared, and the grasshoppers are gone. The sheep are nervous, but still grazing; they do not know what else to do.

And suddenly the light level plummets at a rate visible to the naked eye. Night is falling, and swiftly.

     Totality. The Sun has become a featureless black disk, sharp-edged against a glaring ring that extends as far as the sun itself, flame and fire almost too bright to look at, yet so dim it is normally drowned by the full radiance of the star itself, a radiance so intense it has been known to strike a bare-headed man dead at over ninety million miles. In the rest of the sky, other stars appear, but they are hard to see, or rather, hard to look at. The radiant ring draws the attention, a celestial shout of "Look at me!", a command that cannot be ignored, that must be obeyed. A single sight, sixty seconds of glory, of beauty, of incandescent perfection. A single minute, but worth every second of the six hours of travel to here and back to camp. It might even be worth a three-thousand-dollar hotel room. I understand the people who spend tens of thousands of dollars to experience a total eclipse, who attend every one they can manage, even if they must travel half-way around the world to reach it. And the soul-wrenching disappointment of an eclipse barred, an experience lost, to something as simple and commonplace and uncorrectable as a solid overcast.

The sheep have been baa-ing in baffled bewilderment throughout the darkness, but it was unnoticed in the awe of the minute. Now they are back to grazing. The insects re-emerge, and the light, dim as it is, seems almost back to normal, though less than ten minutes have elapsed since darkness broke. Only now are the birds returning, and with them comes the traffic, as the watchers pack up and abandon the sites they have struggled so long and hard to obtain. They sat rapt and impatient through the growing gloom, but see nothing attractive in the returning light. The day is bright already, much brighter than twilight, but every car displays its lights.

It will be another hour before the moonshadow has fully passed and normal day is restored, but the magic is gone. The slow darkening, the eager anticipation of a unique event, perhaps never to recur for the majority of experiencers, that was magic, that projected a fascination that infected every participant. But it climaxed with totality, and there is no denoument. There is no aftermath. There is no act to follow the magical minute. One single minute to consummate six months of expectation. It is as lame and unprofessional as ending a story "and they lived happily ever after" or "and then he woke up".

But, boy, was it ever worth it!

Starshadow

Yesterday I experienced the wonder of a total solar eclipse. That meant the Moon was as new as it could be; there would be no lunar light at all tonight, not the slightest trace. The sky was clear. What few clouds lined the horizon had dissipated by noon, and no successors appeared all day. Then I awoke a little after midnight, to realize the temperature had fallen below freezing. I was camped in the high montane, on a high plateau, almost a plain, at eighty-four hundred feet, and surrounded by nine-thousand-foot ridges.   There were no settlements in the fifty-mile width of the plateau, nothing but a couple of ski lodges, almost shut down, this being August.   High altitude, clear, dry air, no clouds or haze, no turbulence, no light pollution.   Conditions appeared to be, for once, as perfect as they could be on Earth.   And for once, appearances did not lie.

I set up a chair in which I could recline and look straight up.   I draped a sleeping bag over it, climbed in and zipped up, lit a last cigarette, and lay back to wait for night vision.

The wait was not dull, for even with eyes half-blinded by flashlight and flame, the Milky Way was prominent, and the major constellations were visible.   Cassiopeia was nearly overhead, her husband Cepheus a bit lower (for I was facing northwest), then the Swan and the Dragon, and bright Vega in the Lyre dropping to the horizon, though barely visible to my unadapted eyes.   Andromeda overhead, with Pegasus and Pisces to the left, and to the right, Polaris and traces of the Big Dipper, only partially to be seen through the trees, and dim, being near the horizon.   But in half an hour, the worst of the wait was over.   Stars were discernable right down to the horizon, even dim stars.   The Giraffe was easily seen, one of the few constellations that actually looks like its namesake.   It was a pity the Pleiades were below the horizon, for they would be magnificent on a night such as this; it could be that even the Seventh Sister might show her retiring face.   But there are other wonders to make up for that lack. The nearby Andromeda Galaxy shone clear and bright, the light of two hundred billion suns that had travelled for two and a half million years to entertain me tonight.   I must have pretty good vision to see for two and a half million light-years!

Several travelers wander by.   The slow, stately, barely apparant motion of the low-orbit satellites is just enough to distinguish them from stars. I see several in equatorial orbits, but only in the eastern two-thirds of the sky. In the West, they are in shadow, and therefor invisible. Several high aircraft cross the sky north to south, flying far faster (in apparant motion) than the more distant satellites. And fastest of all are the meteors, streaking in all directions, one every four or five minutes, some so large that they leave a glorious slash across the heavens, a line of light that may persist for more than a second. It is widely believed that fifteen to thirty minutes is all it takes to fully establish night vision. This may be true in most areas, but in a truly dark place, under an uncontaminated sky, on a night that is as dark and as pure as this one, night vision continues to improve for more than an hour. I could not look at my watch without ruining my night-sight, but you know the stars themselves are the most accurate clock in existence, if you know how to read it. The starfield rotates exactly fifteen degrees each hour, and it had moved a bit over twenty degrees before my night vision had reached the point I had been hoping for: I could clearly see the colors of the stars.

Some stars almost always show color, stars of magnitude 0.0 or brighter. Betelgeuse and Sirius are red; Vega and Rigel are blue, or blue-white. Their colors are commonly visible because of their great brightness, because the cones, the color receptors in the eyes, receive enough light to activate. Normal starlight is too weak, after battling its way through our thick and distorting atmosphere, and only triggers the rods, which distinguish light and no-light, and nothing else. But every star is colored. Most are red. Next in commonness are yellow, like our sun. Some are green, or blue. Almost all of the colors of the spectrum are there, but they are very, very difficult to see. Your eyes must be fully adapted to the dark, and there can be no lights, none, to shine across the skies. The air must be very dry, and still, for the slightest turbulence will diffract the light and blend colors together. And the thinner the air, the better the chance that the color will arrive undiminished. Lastly, you have to *look*. To a mere glance, the stars are all white. If you concentrate your attention, if you stare steadily, then you will see the colors. They are dim, somewhat vague, but undeniably there. Red, orange, yellow, green, blue. The color may flicker. The stars may appear to be white eighty percent of the time, especially the dimmer stars. But the brighter stars will show clear color. If you ever see it, you will have no doubts. The colors are real, they are there, it is not your imagination And it is breath-takingly beautiful!

And last comes the culmination. I climbed from my warm nest and stood in the middle of the pale pink-toned dirt road, and looked down. There is a system called the Bortle Scale for classifying the degree of darkness in the night sky. Class 9 is urban, such as the nights of Los Angeles, so bright that only a dozen stars can be seen, if that many. It works down (or up) to rural Class 3 where there is some visible light contamination on the horizon, but the Milky Way is brighter than that loom, and Class 2, which is called "truly dark". There are very, very few places in the continental United States where a Class 2 sky can be experienced. But there is one better, one that no one can count on seeing, for even in the darkest places, the slightest variance from perfect conditions will raise it to Class 2. I had seen Class 1 skies twice, both times in northeast Nevada, in high valleys far from human habitation. And this night I saw it for the third time, the proof, the standard by which Class 1 is defined. There at my feet, faint, diffuse, but clear, strikingly clear when I knelt to get closer, was my shadow, cast by the light of a hundred billion suns, the light of the Milky Way.

Starshadow.

Imagination

Random Patterns

Have you ever listened to the patterns of rainfall? Heard the regularity of the beat of drops, the rhythm of large and small, hard and soft, the subtle cadence, regularity, pattern? I can never quite grasp them, they are forever just out of reach, just *barely* out of reach. You see the pattern in a still pond, you hear the various murmurs of a dancing brook, you watch the rhythmic ripples of wind on long grass, of the sway of tall pines. It lies in all of them, the patterns, the order, the uniformity, but you can never quite grasp them. Why? Why are they ever that one small step, that one miniscule bit beyond your understanding?

Some believe it is a matter of awareness, that your mind is just that little bit too clouded to perceive the truth. I know my awareness has expanded enormously since I first listened to the water-sound decades ago. But in spite of that, there has been no change, and comprehension still eludes me, still lies that infinitesimal thousandth of a nothing beyond my reach. Some say it is perspective, that one must listen and look from just the right angle, from just the right frame of mind. Long ago I used drugs to achieve a more open perspective, and I did hear the words, and I did understand the great hidden concepts. I wrote them down. Later, when my mind was clear, these mystical concepts made no sense: "The rain is only right when it is falling; this is true of all rocks." I no longer use the drugs.

Some will maintain there is no pattern, that the mind has a desire, a need, for regularity, for order, and insists on seeing this order in everything. That desire certainly exists, at least in most people. Consider the faces and shapes we see in clouds and in cliffs. Look at the forests of Germany, the trees planted in neat rectangular arrays, each a uniform distance from the others. Look at most American cities and towns, where equal rectangular blocks predominate. It is orderly. It is efficient. To some, it is even esthetic. At the extreme, we see the person who compulsively straightens picture frames on the wall.

But rain does none of that. It falls when it falls, where it falls, randomly. It needs no uniformity. Wherever it strikes, it spatters, it spreads, it soaks into the ground. The arid dust absorbs it, the thirsty loam passes it on, down to the roots and rocks below. Within a few inches at most, the presence of water is uniform, flowing from greater concentrations to lower, forming, not a pattern, but a ubiquity. Water everywhere, flowing to where it is needed.

So what is the answer, what is the truth? Is "random pattern" an oxymoron, or is randomness a pattern in its own right? Is there meaning in randomness, or is there a truth that lies just beyond what we can sense? Is it nothing, a phantom, an illusion created by our own desires?

I do not know. Perhaps, someday, I will know. For now, I am pleased to have the mystery. You see, I do not *want* to know everything, for if I did, there would be nothing left to learn. How boring omniscience must be! A persons reach must always be greater than his grasp, for otherwise, there would be no point to anything.

Co-Incidence

Things happen. There is no denying it, and no one will dispute it. But sometimes there is the question of whether a thing was caused, intentionally, and who caused it. Like Old Grandfather Live Oak. I wished I could have seen him in his prime, and thirty seconds later, I did. Did Old Grandfather cause it, or direct my attention, or had I seen the younger tree on the way up, and simply not noticed it? Or was it pure chance, did it just happen? Or like happening upon Vedauwoo, driven in by a rainstorm (which stopped as soon as I arrived), and staying a week when I had intended to stay at a later campground, and only overnight at that. Did Vedauwoo call me, or a Muse direct my path? Did I have some spiritual awareness of its existence and allure, some awareness that I was not aware of having? Or was it pure chance, did it just happen? Skeptics are very fond of coincidence; they use it as an explanation for anything they do not want to be true. Whether they realize it or not, what they are saying is simply "The explanation is that there is no explanation". I like to reply to them "There is no such thing as coincidence; those things just happened to occur at the same time". It sort of makes their heads spin.

My bike talks to me. Or, if you prefer, I understand what various sounds and vibrations and motions indicate. Quite similar to, when someone talks to you, you understand what the various sounds and vibrations and motions indicate. I know when she is running hot, or the air filter is getting clogged, or the air pressure in a tire is low. But this time . . . I had not inspected the rear tire recently. I had only six thousand miles on it, and expected to get at least ten. The rear fender makes it difficult to see the tread, and the front tire, easily visible, showed little wear. They usually last about the same distance, and had both been replaced at the same time. So when I felt the mushiness that indicates a low tire, I figured I must have a puncture, and immediately stopped to check. The rear tire was losing air, and I was appalled to see that it was almost bald!

I was only five miles from a town, so I limped in to a tire shop. They did not handle motorcycles, but were happy to fill the tire so I could reach another shop. But in filling the tire, the mechanic found that the valve was leaking. He tightened the stem and finished pumping the tire up, then soaped the tire and found no other leaks I thanked him, and forced a tip on him (he refused to charge anything), and headed off to find a motorcycle service shop to get a new tire.

I was lucky the valve had loosened up at just that time. If it had not, I might have had a blowout at any moment. While not as dangerous as a blowout on a car, especially when it is the rear tire, it would have been a major inconvenience, and I expect it would also have been pretty expensive. Chance? Coincidence? Could be. You are welcome to your opinion, and have my permission to believe whatever you wish (since you will do so regardless). But my opinion is, the bike was warning me. She does that.

Stardust

Fairy dust, elf dust, star dust. They are well known in folk lore and folk legend. They have magical properties that vary from one legend to the next, but always present; these properties are the principal characteristic of the eldritch powder. But what are they? Where do they come from? All myths and legends have a basis in fact, though the fact is generally quite mundane, and all of the magic and fantasy has been appended over the years.

Astrophysicists maintain that at one time, way back in the beginning, all of the matter in the entire universe was hydrogen. Vast clouds of the gas stretched across the light years, dark and unnoticed, because there was no light, and no one to notice it. Eventually these hydrogen atoms began to clump together, drawn by their feeble individual gravities, and the clumps grew, faster and faster as their gravities combined, till the accumulated mass was so great that the internal pressure created temperatures in the millions of degrees. Fahrenheit or centigrade, it does not matter, for these are hyperthermic temperatures. (Hypersonics is the science of sounds too high to be heard. Hyperthermics is the science of temperatures too hot to be felt. Puckish, but true.) At such temperatures the atoms begin to fuse, producing the heavier elements, helium, lithium, boron, and on up through iron, and beyond. Each star (for that is what these hyper-furnaces are) spewed out masses of incandescent particles, mostly hydrogen, but with an admixture of heavier atoms. After a few billion years, when most of the hydrogen was gone, comverted into the heavier elements, the star would explode and strew these heavy atoms throughout surrounding space. More stars formed, more fusion occurred, more and more heavier elements were formed, till eventually, after billions of years (officially) or trillions of years (more likely) our own sun formed, and with it the planets and asteroids and meteoroids and dust, and every last atom of it, except some of the hydrogen, had been a part of some earlier star where it had been manufactured from hydrogen.

Last night I was stargazing. This is a very good place for it. Dry weather, no wind, perfectly clear skies, no local light at all. The only light pollution is a dim glow far to the Northeast. The moon is barely gibbous, but it had set over an hour before. Orion was just rising, all of the Little Dipper stars were visible, and the six main stars of the Pleiades could be easily discerned with the naked eye. And there were meteors, more than I had expected. More meteors than airplanes. Only a few passed overhead each hour, but there were at least a dozen of them for each aircraft. There were fast ones and slow ones, mostly yellow, but a couple of white, and more than one red. Some were so large, they left glowing trails that lingered for more than a second before fading away.

Common knowledge says a meteor glows from the friction of its passage through the atmosphere, but that is incorrect. When a meteor strikes, it, of course, pushes against the air. But it is moving so fast, the air molecules cannot get out of the way, so they are compressed. Just as pumping up a tire heats it from the compression, so does the air in front of a meteor heat up. It gets so hot, it glows. The meteor itself also gets hot, at least on the surface, and begins to melt and vaporize. Eventually the whole rock is heated to gas. We say it has burned up. There may or may not be any actual burning, but without doubt, the rock is now a stream of gas. Vapor. Evaporated and boiled away rock. It cools and condenses into tiny particles of rock, particles so small that they float upon the air, and may take years to finally fall to Earth. You know: Dust. But it does so fall, tons of it, thousands of tons. There are a lot more meteors than just those we see. Most are too small to make a glow bright enough to see from the surface. Many, most of them, are just dust to start with, some moving so slowly that they never glow at all. But all of these particles, the recondensed big ones and the never-melted dust, are falling, drifting down, slowly, so very slowly, but inexorably. There is a rain of dust falling on you right now. Possibly not, if you are indoors. But even then, even in a NASA clean room, you are inhaling bits of stars with every breath you take. You must. You cannot live without it. Every oxygen atom was formed in the heart of a star. Every molecule of your body contains stardust, *is* stardust. Every single plant around me, every blade and bush and tree, every chattering squirrel and twittering bird, every insect, every living thing, is made of stardust. The rocks beneath my feet, the cliffs towering above, the river chatting in its bed, every bit is star-stuff, assembled in stars and scattered across space, to gather here, and grow, and change.

Stardust.

Can you conceive of it *not* being magical?

Insignificance

We were on a mountaintop, gazing at the vast forest spread below us, at the steep valleys bordering streams, the occasional meadows and glades, the hawks circling above and the deer grazing below, when my companion said "It makes you feel so small and insignificant".

What a strange concept! This is Life, this is the World! I am not separate, I am a part of it, just as I am also a part, not separate, of Humanity. We, and I, have the power to destroy it, by plan or by accident. We have the wisdom, many of us, to withhold that power, to preserve Life. We remove diseased trees, and light controlled fires to clear away accumulated debris so that wildfire will not kill everything. We kill or drive off predators to protect our livestock, then take on the role and duties of the predators to keep the prey from over-populating. We make mistakes, but, usually, do our best to remedy them. We can, through ignorance and greed, cause great damage. We can, through education and compassion, repair and preserve.

At one time, the United States, from the Atlantic to the Mississippi and beyond, was one vast forest. That forest is largely gone, replaced with fields and pastures, but there is just as much life, and the great forests of the western mountains are still there, and protected. The face of the world has changed, in no small way.

I do not feel small or insignificant; I feel powerful and responsible. The world is change; even the rocks know that. Life is self-directed change. Humanity is conscious, planned, self-directed change. We have more power to create and to destroy than any other life. We have the awareness of this power and at least a partial understanding of the consequences; we certainly understand there *will* be consequences.

I feel an obligation and a duty to preserve and enhance Life and the World. I want you to feel this also, but I cannot force them upon you, for the only valid duties and obligations are those the individual willingly takes upon himself. Please, educate yourself. *Look* at the world. Feel it. Understand and accept that you are a part of it, whether you wish it or not. You are neither small nor insignificant. Destroy life or preserve it, what you do unto others, you do unto yourself.

About the Author

The Lonesome Hillbilly is a wanderer from birth. Born in the Lone Star Republic (but not in Texas), he traveled a thousand miles by his first birthday, and ten thousand by his second. He lives on a motorcycle, and in a tent he made. He has been in every state of the Union, plus Asia and Europe. Politically he

is a Rational Anarchist. Spiritually, he respects all religions, and no churches. He winters in the low deserts of Arizona, and tours all New Mexico during the Spring. The rest of the time, you will find him somewhere within five hundred miles of the Rocky Mountains. Probably.

Stay Free!